W9-CLG-909

Bloom's

GUIDES

Ray Bradbury's
Fahrenheit 451

The Adventures of Huckleberry Finn
All the Pretty Horses
Animal Farm
Beloved
Brave New World
The Catcher in the Rye
The Chosen
The Crucible
Cry, the Beloved Country
Death of a Salesman
Fahrenheit 451
The Glass Menagerie
The Grapes of Wrath
Great Expectations
The Great Gatsby
Hamlet
The Handmaid's Tale
The House on Mango Street
I Know Why the Caged Bird Sings
The Iliad
Lord of the Flies
Macbeth
Maggie: A Girl of the Streets
The Member of the Wedding
The Metamorphosis
Of Mice and Men
1984
The Odyssey
One Hundred Years of Solitude
Pride and Prejudice
Ragtime
Romeo and Juliet
Slaughterhouse-Five
The Scarlet Letter
Snow Falling on Cedars
A Streetcar Named Desire
A Tale of Two Cities
The Things They Carried
To Kill a Mockingbird

Bloom's
GUIDES

Ray Bradbury's
Fahrenheit 451

Edited & with an Introduction
by Harold Bloom

CHELSEA HOUSE
PUBLISHERS
An imprint of Infobase Publishing

Bloom's Guides: Fahrenheit 451

Copyright ©2007 by Infobase Publishing
Introduction ©2007 by Harold Bloom

Chelsea House
An imprint of Infobase Publishing
132 West 31st Street
New York NY 10001

Library of Congress Cataloging-in-Publication Data
Ray Bradbury's Fahrenheit 451 / Harold Bloom, editor.
  p. cm. — (Bloom's guides)
Includes bibliographical references and index.
ISBN 0-7910-9294-1 (hardcover)
1. Bradbury, Ray, 1920- Fahrenheit 451. 2. Science fiction, American—History and criticism. 3. Book burning in literature. I. Bloom, Harold. II. Title: Farenheit 451. III. Series.

PS3503.R167F3363 2006
813'.54—dc22   2006031095

Contributing Editor: Michael Cisco
Cover design by Takeshi Takahashi

Printed in the United States of America

Bang EJB 10 9 8 7 6 5 4 3 2 1

This book is printed on acid-free paper.

you cannot read Shakespeare and his peers, then you
memory, and if you cannot remember, then you will
to think.

y, though his work is of the surface, will survive as a
st. "The house will crumble and the books will burn,"
vens mournfully prophesied, but a saving remnant
e a new party of Memory. In our America-to-come,
Memory will become the party of Hope, a reversal of
terms but hardly of Emersonian values. Is there a
brise now than stimulating coming generations to
emory the best that has been written?

Contents

Introduction

reading. If
will forfeit
not be able
Bradbu
moral fabuli
Wallace Ste
will constitu
the party of
Emersonian
higher enter
commit to m

While *Fahrenheit 451* manifes
thin, rather tendentious nov
somewhat diverse periods. I
the Cold War of the 1950s
1960s and has not lost its re
millennium. One does not
Theological Age to overv
George W. Bush's procl
decision without consultin
be no books to burn. In th
read Shakespeare or Dant

I resort to a merely p
the New British Libr
instauration, and invited
congratulatory week. At
to make a third, in co
authorities on software
protested that I did no
nothing of software (ha
that my function woul
compliment and the in
once-great library was

Reading *Fahrenh*
novel its stereotype
prophetic hope tha
answer. When I tea
my students to read
and over again unt
memory. *Myself*, I
trope), and I repea
day. Bradbury, a ha
the age of the Sc

Biographical Sketch

One of the more celebrated and prolific authors of genre fiction, Ray Bradbury has, in his long career, produced many enduringly popular works of horror, fantasy, and science fiction. A literary creator of unusual flexibility and breadth, he is particularly credited with the renovation of science fiction, and the elevation of literary standards in what had been often dismissed as mere pulp trash. Largely by virtue of his poetic prose and his instinctive gift for discovering points of intersection between speculative thinking and emotional poignancy, he proved again that genre fiction could be as profound as any other variety.

Ray Douglas Bradbury was born in Waukegan, Illinois, August 22, 1920. His great-grandfather and grandfather were both in the newspaper business, while his father worked for a telephone company. Bradbury makes constant recourse to nostalgic images of his boyhood in Illinois throughout his work. Their residence in Waukegan was interrupted twice, on both occasions for a single year only, 1926-27 and 1932-33, during which times the family resided in Tucson, Arizona. Some critics have speculated that Bradbury's evocative descriptions of alien worlds, and especially his conjurations of the Mars in *The Martian Chronicles*, may have originated in his encounter with the unusual desert landscape of Arizona.

In 1934, the Bradbury family relocated permanently to Los Angeles, California, where Ray Bradbury has lived ever since. Four years later, he graduated from Los Angeles High School and, as was not unusual at the time, decided to forgo attending university. Instead he sold newspapers on the street and read copiously, sensationalistic pulp science fiction, fantasy, and horror stories being the staple if not the only element in his literary diet. It was around this time that he began trying his hand at writing his own stories, some of which were accepted and printed without compensation to the author. Bradbury received his first payment for a story in 1941, for a piece which appeared in *Super Science Stories*. He continued to apply himself to his work with a steady diligence that would become one of his more widely recognized traits as an author.

Eventually, he had accumulated a sufficient number of horror or darkly-themed stories to assemble his first anthology, and first book. This was *Dark Carnival*, published in 1947 by Arkham House, a company based in Wisconsin and which was initially founded to promote the works of another American master of the weird tale, H.P. Lovecraft. It was also in 1947 that Bradbury married Marguerite McClure, who was destined to remain his wife until her death fifty-six years later, in 2003. Together they would have four children, all daughters.

Bradbury's next book, a collection of linked stories all set on Mars, appeared in 1950, and it was arguably this title, *The Martian Chronicles*, that established him as a writer and forever linked his name specifically to science fiction. His next collection, *The Illustrated Man*, 1951, was also well-received. Between 1951 and 1954, more than two dozen of Bradbury's stories reached a wider audience in comic adaptations published by EC Comics. Radio listeners would have known Bradbury's work, including many of the episodes of *The Martian Chronicles*, through adaptations for such programs as X Minus One, Suspense, and Lights Out. His work first began to appear on television at this time as well, and was featured on the CBS Television Workshop and Alfred Hitchcock Presents, among others. Two films, both released within a few weeks of each other in 1953, were also Bradbury adaptations: "It Came From Outer Space" (from "The Meteor") and "The Beast From 20,000 Fathoms" (from "The Fog Horn").

It was also in 1953 that Bradbury's first novel (technically speaking) *Fahrenheit 451* was published to considerable acclaim. The bulk of Bradbury's most celebrated and influential works of fiction were published in the fifties and early sixties; following *Fahrenheit 451* were another horror anthology, *The October Country* (1955), and his second novel, *Dandelion Wine* (1957), for which Dandelion Crater, on earth's moon, is named. (Years later, an asteroid, Bradbury 9766, was named in his honor as well.)

With the 1960s and 1970s came more and somewhat higher profile adaptations of Bradbury's work: Francois Truffaut directed *Fahrenheit 451*, and *The Illustrated Man* was transformed into an episodic film in 1968. *Something Wicked This Way Comes* was cinematized in 1981. In all, more than thirty-five films and television productions have been produced based on Bradbury's stories, for which he was awarded a star on the Hollywood Walk of Fame. *The Martian Chronicles* aired on television as miniseries in 1980, and, five years later, The Ray Bradbury Theater, featuring Bradbury's own adaptations of his work for television, commenced what would prove to be a run of seven seasons presenting 65 of Bradbury's stories.

Bradbury's steady pace of publication has not slackened in over sixty years. Most critics feel his later work, from the late 1980's to the present, does not compare well with his landmark earlier writings, but this later work is still consistently well received. On November 17, 2004, George W. and Laura Bush honored Bradbury with the National Medal of Arts at a White House ceremony. In addition to this distinction, Bradbury has been the recipient of lifetime achievement awards presented by the World Fantasy committee and the Stoker award committee, a First Fandom Award, and an Emmy for "The Halloween Tree." He is a Grand Master of the Science Fiction Writers of America and living inductee to the Science Fiction Hall of Fame.

The Story Behind the Story

Fahrenheit 451 was written when what would come to be known as the "McCarthy era" was in its earliest stages of development. While he had not yet founded the infamous House Un-American Activities Committee, Wisconsin Senator Joseph McCarthy had already inflamed public opinion with an unsubstantiated (and never proven) allegation that Communist spies had somehow insinuated themselves into the State Department. Labeled a "witch hunter" by his critics, McCarthy promoted his political position by fostering an atmosphere of suspicion and insecurity, while remaining studiously vague about what a "Communist" might actually be.

Early in 1953, America's foremost playwright at the time, Arthur Miller, published *The Crucible*. On the surface, the play was Miller's account of the Salem witch trials, but many understood it as a thinly veiled critique of McCarthy's tactics. While Miller did not address "McCarthyism" in his play, which was more preoccupied with the narrowness and paranoia of Puritan New England, the term "witch trial" would later come to be applied to McCarthy's public hearings.

While not a leftist in his own political leanings, Bradbury unflaggingly supported the cause of civil liberties and opposed both overt and subtler censorship. Like many of his contemporaries in the early fifties, he was concerned with the development of authoritarian politics. Memories of Nazi atrocities were still fresh at the time, and many were worried that, in the course of fighting the "Cold War" with the Soviet Union, the United States would so consistently promote an exaggerated idea of security over the personal liberties of its citizens as to become a Soviet-style police state itself. More thoughtful observers, like Bradbury, noticed too the less obvious ways in which conformity, reasonableness, and skepticism could be used to smooth over the obvious brutality of a fascistic regime.

George Orwell's famous novel *Nineteen Eighty-Four*, a date he came to simply by inverting the last two digits of the year in which he began to write the novel, was widely read and highly influential in its stark depiction of a supposedly benevolent, actually authoritarian state. Its depiction of a prison-like society in which any individual could be placed under surveillance at any time for no reason became the most powerful image of oppression in twentieth-century literature.

Bradbury's own vision of a totalitarian future was arguably even more deeply influenced by Aldous Huxley's 1932 novel, *Brave New World*, to which Orwell's dystopia formed a pendant. Huxley envisioned a future in which people were controlled by pleasure, treats, and little indulgences doled out by an invisible, unaccountable government. Huxley's citizens were eugenically engineered and stratified according to a strict system into basically normal Alphas, less intelligent Betas and so on.

Fahrenheit 451 was composed in 1952 and published the following year. The nuclear arms race was well on its way when in 1952, England announced to the world that it possessed an atomic bomb, and the US conducted secret tests of a new, vastly more powerful weapon, the hydrogen bomb, in the Bikini atoll. The successful detonation of the "H-bomb" was reported in the first few days of 1953. Many people observed the proliferation of nuclear weapons, and their increasing power, with deep misgivings—uncertain where this escalation of destructive power might lead.

Given the political climate of the time, *Fahrenheit 451* was a popular book and one of the most well-received in Bradbury's career. He was immediately regarded as belonging to a small but important unofficial group of writers who were bringing to science fiction a new level of literary and intellectual sophistication, bringing it to bear on a world in which the rate of change, driven by unprecedented developments in technology, was rapidly accelerating. Bradbury, like many, found these developments heartening, even thrilling, but did not shy away from their darker implications. Since its publication, *Fahrenheit 451* has joined *Nineteen Eight-Four* on a short list of classic anti-totalitarian literature. Renowned French director François Truffaut adapted it for the screen in 1967, and it has remained in print for over fifty years.

List of Characters

Guy Montag, named, as Bradbury confesses in his afterword, for the Montag paper mill, is the pivotal character, whose intellectual awakening defines the trajectory of the novel. He is at first a thoughtless conformist, whose obedience is more a matter of sociability, good fellowship, and a sense of duty. There is no trace of the intellectual about him; Bradbury's point, in making Montag the hero of his novel, is that anyone, even someone who could be mistaken for a jackbooted thug, can change.

Mildred Montag, Guy's wife, is a timid, mentally-numb drab. She is fascinated by a vague, unreal vision of happiness that can only be found on television, which she watches incessantly. Her near-death, an unreal accident resulting from an overdose of legal drugs intended to make her happy seems to point to the mental and spiritual death threatening Guy.

The teenage girl, **Clarisse McClellan**, is an anomaly. She exhibits a curiosity about the world around her, particularly the natural world, and a philosophical propensity. Her perceptive questions set Guy on a path of escalating uncertainty about the purpose of his work, the values of his civilization, and the meaning of his life. Although Clarisse is a sunny, unembittered young woman, her thoughtfulness makes others, even her parents, uncomfortable. Montag is surprised to discover a person who does not set the highest premium on fitting in.

The one-time professor of English, **Faber**, is a sullen loner who becomes a hesitant co-conspirator with Guy, rejecting his abortive plan to destroy the fire brigade from within by planting books in other firemen's houses and becoming in effect a second self to Montag. Faber is fearful, and cautious, but determined.

Montag's supervisor, **Captain Beatty**, is the nominal villain of the novel, corresponding to Orwell's O'Brien. Not quite the wild-eyed fanatic one might expect, Beatty was himself once very interested in books, and felt in himself intimations of the questioning spirit that has taken root in Montag. But Beatty rejected reflection and critique as evils, producing nothing but confusion and weakness, and so embraced the destruction of books. His character alternately reflects the fearsome power of the state and its seemingly reasonable, accommodating side.

Granger leads an underground resistance society of intellectuals, who form a living library of memorized books. They have abandoned the state and live a nomadic existence on its periphery. The novel affords Granger little time to be fleshed out as a fully-realized character, but it is clear that his leadership is reliable and his willingness to accept Montag is a sign of the latter's redemption.

Summary and Analysis

Bradbury created *Fahrenheit 451* by expanding one of his short stories, entitled "The Fireman." The novel describes what in literary parlance is called a "dystopia," that is, an imaginary state or civilization in which true happiness is impossible. Dystopias are usually caricatures of the writer's own society, set in a near future in which the negative qualities the writer perceives in the present are permitted to run amok, so that the representation he creates exemplifies the consequences of a current set of circumstances run out to their logical conclusion.

Fahrenheit 451 is a dystopian novel set in what appears to be the United States in the twenty-fourth century. The government has become a subtly resourceful despotism sheltering itself behind comforting fictions generated by a gigantically overdeveloped electronic media. These illusions are broadcast in all manner of ways, but Bradbury particularly emphasizes the importance of television: most homes come equipped with several television screens, large enough to cover entire walls. Multiple screens can be employed to create virtually three-dimensional, wholly encompassing televised environments for viewers. The programming is simplistic and subject to extremely rapid alterations, designed to keep citizens entertained, content, tractable, distracted, and divided. Linguistic sophistication and complexity have been reduced to facilitate mass manipulation, and to this end, all books are banned. Possession of any written matter is a felony punishable by death. The "fireman" no longer extinguishes fires in Bradbury's dystopia, but, in an Orwellian inversion of the meaning of the word, now sets fires, specifically to burn books. The title of the novel refers to the temperature at which paper burns.

Fire is the most important symbol in the novel. Bradbury will invoke fire in many forms, time and again, because it has a double nature. In the first case, fire is one of the principle tools of human civilization, by means of which human beings were first able to function at night or in places inaccessible to sunlight, or in cold climates; fire is essential to the hygienic preparation of food, a deterrent to the approach of predators, and can be employed to send simple signals over long distances. The Greek myth of Prometheus, often invoked in science fiction, helps to make clear the importance of fire: Prometheus, the creator of mankind and yet not himself a god, steals fire from the gods, who guard it jealously for themselves, and gives it to mankind, to help them survive. For this transgression against the gods, Prometheus is severely punished, and this punishment points to the second aspect of fire. While fire is useful, it is also dangerous, and can, if not carefully controlled, become a destroyer. Especially important is the power fire possesses to grow without limitation.

In a synecdoche, Bradbury will make fire the symbol of all human technology. This technology, like fire, can vastly increase man's power, but it can also exceed the capacity of mankind to control it, and so become a destroyer. This symbolism is especially acute with reference to nuclear weapons, which were widely regarded as a kind of demonic fire, powerful enough to destroy the entire world. The state abuses fire and technology to destroy, to intrude, to spy, to dazzle and delude, to make war, to enslave. But the fire at the end also destroys them and escapes their control.

What is the counter-force that makes the control of fire, or technology, possible? For Bradbury, the contrary is simply humanity itself, which is symbolized in *Fahrenheit 451* not so much by individual human beings, as by books themselves. It might be said that the book is an image of humanity as such, and a reverence for books is a reverence for humanity. Books, for Bradbury, are the legacy of what was, the remnant of once-lived experience, the embodiment of the idealized humanity of his character, Clarisse McClellan. Human beings live and die, come and go, they may even become inhuman; the purpose of the book, for Bradbury, is to prevent this loss of humanity by reminding the reader of the true nature of the human condition.

The first of the novel's three segments, **The Hearth and the Salamander**, introduces Bradbury's protagonist, Guy

Montag, who is in most respects a typical, dutiful fireman, who performs his function diligently and without any particular curiosity about it. He is a product of this civilization and, as one would expect, he takes its values for granted. As the story opens, Montag returns to his suburban home after another ordinary day of book burning, only to discover his wife, Mildred, at death's door. She has accidentally taken an overdose of medication meant to make her happy, and Montag has barely enough time to call in medical assistance.

> They had two machines ... One of them slid down your stomach like a black cobra down an echoing well looking for all the old water and the old time gathered there ...

The other drains Mildred completely of her poisoned blood, and replaces it with new blood. Montag is warmly reassured by the medical technicians that Mildred's memory of her suicide attempt, if in fact it was one, has been wiped away. This sequence of events not only introduces the reader to a character caught up in an escalating, life-threatening escape from reality, it also in effect makes Mildred part of an extended mechanism of the state. She is almost always physically and mentally connected to some form of machinery that seems to be sucking the life out of her and replacing it with a worthless substitute.

As in *Brave New World*, the state in *Fahrenheit 451* manipulates citizens with recreational pharmaceuticals. When the novel was written, barbiturates and other drugs were commonly prescribed for only nominally medical purposes; "tranquilizers," "diet pills," and the like were more commonly taken for psychological relief than for the alleviation of any physical ailment. Mildred feels it would be wrong of her to admit her unhappiness, as this would be tantamount to expressing ingratitude toward the state, which, it is taken as axiomatic, is an ideal state, creating perfect happiness. Unable to admit ultimately even to herself that she is deeply unhappy, Mildred plunges into the sprawling, brightly-colored, beguiling but finally empty fantasies of a monolithic electronic media operated by the state. Every home in Bradbury's world is outfitted with colossal television screens whose function goes far beyond entertainment; Mildred, who represents the helpless, fascinated subjects of the state, understands herself virtually. She exists only as mediated by television, but, because television can offer only intangible images, no matter how exhilarating an escape it may provide, it cannot truly satisfy the profounder needs of her human nature. In her confusion and self-misunderstanding, Mildred can think of no better answer to her mounting, unacknowledged anxiety and failure to achieve anything in herself commensurate with the phony bliss she sees on her television screen, than to watch more and more television and to take greater and greater amounts of the drug that is meant to make her happy. Plainly the two, the drug and the television, are aspects of the same palliative strategy of the state. Even the newspaper Mildred reads consists of nothing but images.

Mildred's overdose is the culmination of a spiralling cycle of drugging and denial, and, once she is revived by medical machinery, this cycle appears to begin all over again. Not only is her behavior itself mechanical, but there is a strong implication that she is in effect a zombie, that her resuscitation was an illusion, and she exists in a technologically-mediated living death. Montag has taken his marriage largely for granted. He does not love his wife so much as assume he loves his wife, simply because she is his wife. Likewise, he assumes that she loves him. When confronted with the prospect of her death, he is shocked to discover he doesn't really know Mildred; nearly losing her causes him to confront the fact that he can't say, clearly or vaguely, just whom it was he might have lost. He does not have her to lose. Arguably worse, from Montag's point of view, is Mildred's basic indifference to him. His identity, his individuality, means nothing to her; he is simply her husband. Anyone else could fulfill the same role for her, and she would be as satisfied as she is with Montag. Her near-suicide has the effect of compelling Montag to realize that his marriage to Mildred is a sham.

19

This discovery does not fully register with Montag right away, and in the meantime he is prevented from returning to his former, more comfortable condition by the appearance in his life of Clarisse McClellan, a teenaged girl living in the neighborhood whose path crosses his largely by chance.

Clarisse is an unusual young lady for her time, with an innocent penchant for wondering about the world around her, and a preference for the natural and the thought-provoking as opposed to the artificial and the mind-numbing. Through her, the reader learns about the condition of younger people in Bradbury's dystopia: she complains that her friends keep shooting each other, dying in fights, violent accidents, and even in games. This is an extension of the simulated violence and controlled recklessness of mid-twentieth century theme parks and entertainment, with all restraints removed and all disapproval vanished. Bradbury seems to anticipate a future in which parents will abandon their children indifferently to their fates, to be raised by a technocratic state machinery which turns them into amoral, violent, thrillseeking barbarians— precisely the opposite of the civilizing and upbuilding role traditionally attributed to education.

To an extent, Clarisse may be said to represent a natural and spontaneous, pre-intellectual human propensity toward observation and reflection. Her thoughtfulness is contagious, it seems, and Montag, after meeting her serendipitously in his neighborhood and subsequent random run-ins with her, begins to question his own circumstances in an apolitical, extremely simple way. All his life he has been indirectly discouraged from thinking by a state which does not and cannot openly say why it discourages thought, as this would involve an open admission of tyranny and therefore subject the state to the risk of rebellion by ruining its pretense of honesty and disinterested good will.

While he has no word for it, Montag plainly has fallen in love with Clarisse. Bradbury does not say this in so many words inasmuch as he intimates it in the language he employs to represent Montag's feelings for Clarisse:

He saw himself in her eyes, suspended in two shining drops of bright water, himself dark and tiny, in fine detail, the lines about his mouth, everything there, as if her eyes were two miraculous bits of violet amber that might capture and hold him intact. Her face, turned to him now, was fragile milk crystal with a soft and constant light in it. It was not the hysterical light of electricity but—what? But the strangely comfortable and rare and gently flattering light of the candle. One time, as a child, in a power-failure, his mother had found and lit a last candle and there had been a brief hour of rediscovery, of such illumination that space lost its vast dimensions and drew comfortably around them, and they, mother and son alone, transformed, hoping that the power might not come on again too soon ...

Bradbury contends that Romantic love, far from being a historical invention, is in fact an innate and inborn human emotion; he does not argue this, but the spontanaeity with which Montag breaks into a poetic language highly unlikely for a man of his background seems to point to this contention. As at all important moments of self-discovery in *Fahrenheit 451*, fire appears in this passage; specifically, the intimate, gentle, feminine flame of the candle, which is the traditional light by which one reads in the dark. This is the fire, not of passion— Montag's love for Clarisse is too abstract to be sexual—but of a tender, infantile feeling not unlike the love he remembers feeling for his mother. Where electric light is "hysterical," showing too much and overloading the senses, the candle shows only what is immediately at hand, and that indistinctly, so that the world seems smaller, simpler, and therefore more "comfortable." The light from Clarisse's face emerges from water, from milk, from crystal; it is organic, basic, and natural. Montag's sentiments toward women adopt, as it were reflexively, a tendency to see women as simple, natural, and nurturing.

Bradbury's dystopia is supposed, in its own words, to be a very happy and comfortable place; Montag will discover, in many different ways, that this is a lie. The house Montag calls home is, like all other suburban houses, an automatic house, which coolly and efficiently cleans and maintains itself, doing everything for its inhabitants so that they often find they have nothing to do.

> ... the room was cold but nonetheless he felt he could not breathe. He did not wish to open the curtains and open the french windows, for he did not want the moon to come into the room. So, with the feeling of a man who will die in the next hour for lack of air, he felt his way toward his open, separate, and therefore cold bed.

Mildred is not simply a housewife, she is strongly identified with the coldness and automaticity of the house. The thematic fire of the novel has burned itself out in such places, leaving behind a cold and sterile shell. In contrast to Clarisse McClellan, Mildred is unorganic and inert, a simulacrum of a woman.

The third significant occasion in this escalating sequence of destabilizations and disillusionments comes when Montag is called upon to destroy the home of an old woman who hoards books. From Montag's original point of view, such disobedience to the law is absolutely incomprehensible. The question of where the books come from seems unimportant to him. The destruction by fire of homes containing books is not unusual, but in this case the old woman takes matters into her own hands by setting the fire herself, and remaining in the house to die in the flames. The mysteries of books—where they come from, why anyone would value them, even under the risks attached to the possession of books by the state—are already beginning to trouble Montag in minor ways. He cannot fathom why anyone would risk death to possess books, but this is after all a fate that could conceivably be avoided by an astute, criminal book collector. But this, an actual, spectacular death, stuns Montag. The results of the old woman's act are no different than what would have occurred had she submitted passively to the state: her books are burned, and she is dead. Montag is fundamentally shaken not so much by these results but by the display of individual initiative and power by the old woman. Instead of submitting to the state and its power of life and death, she took that power to herself. The old woman's defiance unto death is a kind of martyrdom that is entirely at odds with, and therefore throws into stark relief, the powerlessness of the model citizen. Deeply shaken, Montag retrieves, almost without thinking, one of the old woman's books, and takes it home. It turns out that this is not the only book in his possession, that he has been secreting books in his home.

This episode would give rise to a minor controversy among critics, who felt that the old woman's reference to "Master Ridley," meaning Nicholas Ridley, an Anglican bishop of the seventeenth century who was burned at the stake for opposing censorship of dissenters, was too obscure and reflected a general tendency in the novel to introduce self-importantly abstruse and elevated allusions for their own sake. A number of critics pointedly argued that Bradbury was simply sprinkling learned citations through the novel in an implausible and contrived way. However, Bradbury's position was plainly that the quality of literature is an innate property of the work itself, and that the critical reader is above all reverencing the work.

They said nothing on their way back to the firehouse. Nobody looked at anyone else. Montag sat in the front seat with Beatty and Black. They did not even smoke their pipes. They sat there looking out the front of the great salamander as they turned a corner and went silently on.

"Master Ridley," said Montag at last.

"What?" said Beatty.

"She said, 'Master Ridley.' She said some crazy thing when we came in the door. 'Play the man,' she said, 'Master Ridley. Something, something, something.'"

"We shall this day light such a candle, by God's grace, in England, as I trust shall never be put out," said

Beatty. Stoneman glanced over at the Captain, as did Montag, startled.

Beatty rubbed his chin. "A man named Latimer said that to a man named Nicholas Ridley, as they were being burnt alive at Oxford, for heresy, on October 16, 1555."

Shortly after this episode, Montag learns that Clarisse McClellan has been liquidated by the state. A nameless functionary somewhere had decided evidently that she was, in concurrence with Captain Beatty's term for her, a ticking "time bomb" of subversion waiting to go off. So she was denied the chance. With this news, and in light of the experiences he has lately undergone, Montag falls into deep despondency, entirely unsure of who he is and of his values. Mildred remarks a change in her husband's character, but only distractedly. She doesn't care about, or for that matter even notice, him enough to raise suspicions. The television world in which she persists in immersing herself has long ago become the highest and truest reality she knows. However, Montag's neglect of his work brings on a visit from his supervisor, the fire chief Captain Beatty, who is reminiscent of Orwell's O'Brien. Unlike O'Brien, however, Captain Beatty has only a superficial mind and seems honestly to embrace the bogus history and anti-intellectual ideology of the state, whose rhetoric he transparently emits.

"When did it all start, you ask, this job of ours, how did it come about, where, when? Well, I'd say it really got started around about a thing called the Civil War. Even though our rule book claims it was founded earlier. The fact is we didn't get along well until photography came into its own. Then—motion pictures in the early Twentieth Century. Radio. Television. Things began to have *mass*."

Montag sat in bed, not moving

"And because they had mass, they became simpler," said Beatty. "Once, books appealed to a few people, here, there, everywhere. They could afford to be different. The world was roomy. But then the world got full of eyes and elbows and mouths. Double, triple, quadruple population. Films and radios, magazines, books, leveled down to a sort of paste-pudding norm, do you follow me?"

"I think so."

Beatty peered at the smoke pattern he had put out on the air. "'Picture it. Nineteenth-century man with his horses, dogs, carts, slow motion. Then, in the Twentieth Century, speed up your camera. Books cut shorter. Condensations. Digests. Tabloids. Everything boils down to the gag, the snap ending."

"Snap ending." Mildred nodded.

"Classics cut to fifteen-minute radio shows, then cut again to fill a two-minute book column, winding up at last as a ten or twelve-line dictionary résumé. I exaggerate, of course. The dictionaries were for reference. But many of those whose sole knowledge of *Hamlet* (you know the title certainly, Montag; it is probably only a faint rumor of a title to you, Mrs. Montag) whose sole knowledge, as I say, of *Hamlet* was a one-page digest in a book that claimed: *now at last you can read all the classics; keep up with your neighbors.* Do you see? Out of the nursery into the college and back to the nursery; there's your intellectual pattern for the past five centuries or more."

It is in the speeches of Beatty that Bradbury's subtlest points begin to emerge. Books were not merely banned, but initially subjected to a historical process of compression that parallels the compression of mankind into the confinement of cities. This process is attributed to history by Beatty, but he describes it in an entirely ahistorical way, as if it were a kind of natural event, akin to a shift in weather patterns. Beatty glosses over the role that individuals, and thought itself, for that matter, play in the development of human history, so there is no questioning why this acceleration takes place, or how or why the human population grows so rapidly or is so compressed in space. Most important of all, here Beatty, who presents himself as one of the boys, and a man of the people, reveals his real anti-populism. Books did not, he argues, become simplified because the government was trying to make its citizenry more stupid, but because the people themselves rejected sophisticated literature in favor of quicker thrills.

"Speed up the film, Montag, quick. *Click, Pic, Look, Eye, Now, Flick, Here, There, Swift, Pace, Up, Down, In, Out, Why, How, Who, What, Where, Eh?, Uh!, Bang!, Smack!, Wallop, Bing, Bong, Boom!* Digest-digests, digest-digest-digests. Politics? One column, two sentences, a headline! Then, in midair, all vanishes! Whirl man's mind around so fast under the pumping hands of publishers, exploiters, broadcasters that the centrifuge flings off all unnecessary, time-wasting thought!"

This is one of the aspects of what is known as technocracy: a form of state organization which places expediency and efficiency above the expressed desires of the community. The state does not claim to possess a superior ideology, but only a superior means of operation, without what is "unnecessary, time-wasting." The questions why the state operates at all, what it's for, or whether or not efficiency and expediency are worth the sacrifices made to attain them, are prevented from arising.

"Number one: Do you know why books such as this are so important? Because they have quality. And what does the word quality mean? To me it means texture. This book has *pores*. It has features. This book can go under the microscope. You'd find life under the glass, streaming past in infinite profusion. The more pores, the more truthfully recorded details of life per square inch you can get on a sheet of paper, the more 'literary' you are. That's *my* definition anyway. *Telling detail.*

Fresh detail. The good writers touch life often. The mediocre ones run a quick hand over her. The bad ones rape her and leave her for the flies.

"So now do you see why books are hated and feared? They show the pores in the face of life. The comfortable people want only wax moon faces, poreless, hairless, expressionless. We are living in a time when flowers are trying to live on flowers, instead of growing on good rain and black loam. Even fireworks, for all their prettiness, come from the chemistry of the earth. Yet somehow we think we can grow, feeding on flowers and fireworks, without completing the cycle back to reality....

In a striking use of irony, it is through Beatty that Bradbury speaks most directly in *Fahrenheit 451*. Books are not so much banned by the state as by the people, who find they are made uncomfortable by them. Comfort is associated by Bradbury with velocity: it is easier to take in the world when images succeed each other at great speed, so that the observer is able to absorb only fleeting outlines. Books must be read slowly and carefully, with the complete attention of the reader carefully gathered and steadily fixed on a series of well-chosen moments. For Bradbury, this point of view alone is sufficient to guarantee a more thoughtful, less selfish observer. A reader must in effect adopt an attitude of thoughtful reflection in order to read at all. Beatty believes that thoughtful reflection is never pleasurable; that it is always painful and difficult.

The zipper displaces the button and a man lacks just that much time to think while dressing at dawn, a philosophical hour, and thus a melancholy hour....

... We stand against the small tide of those who want to make everyone unhappy with conflicting theory and thought. We have our fingers in the dike. Hold steady. Don't let the torrent of melancholy and drear philosophy drown our world ....

...We all must be alike. Not everyone born free and equal, as the Constitution says, but everyone *made* equal. Each man the image of every other; then all are happy, for there are no mountains to make them cower, to judge themselves against. So! A book is a loaded gun in the house next door. Burn it. (58)

The thoughtful observer notices differences, and introduces carefully reasoned distinctions between things. But Beatty believes that human beings are too lazy and stupid to manage such distinctions, or to enjoy any sense of accomplishment in creating them well. The state, on the other hand, deals only with masses and remains indifferent to the individual except insofar as the individual interferes with the smooth operation of its handling of the mass. This is why individuality must be suppressed, according to Beatty, and the distinctions between human beings reduced to a manageable minimum. Beatty's chilling definition of happiness reduces it to a condition of supreme complacency, such that the "happy citizen" cannot even conceive of a better state.

Beatty relates to Montag the official history of the firemen, an ahistorical mish-mash which claims that Benjamin Franklin founded the first fire company (he did, but it was designed, as all contemporary fire departments are, to extinguish fires) in 1790 to purge the colonies of Royalist propaganda. Beatty suggests that it is their high purpose to defend the simple people around them from the pernicious lies of unspecified enemies external to the state and oddly one-dimensional subversives within the state. In either case, the enemies or the subversives are represented as mindlessly evil and destructive people, without histories or reasons for what they do, and who have nothing of the slightest value to say. Beatty also suggests that to listen to them at all is to risk becoming irrevocably lost. He states that a strong state listens to no one, but, like a computer, simply and uniformly imposes a blind grid of values, also not specified but, needless to say, entirely "good" and "democratic," on all. In Beatty's world nobody likes reading, and, with the development of electronic media and the ready propagation of images, print media is obsolete and useless making those who cling to books Luddite fools, subversives, who are outsiders and are insane and dangerous.

> But the public," [Beatty rhapsodizes,] "knowing what it wanted, spinning happily, let the comic books survive. And the three-dimensional sex magazines, of course. There you have it, Montag. It didn't come from the government down. There was no dictum, no declaration, no censorship, to start with, no! Technology, mass exploitation, and minority pressure carried the trick, thank God.

The firehouse comes equipped with a monstrous robotic creature, a kind of embodiment of state power, called the "Mechanical Hound." This being actually bears far less resemblance to a dog than to a spider, which makes Beatty's use of the word "spinning" in the passage above suggestive. The state is embodied in a spider, and the action whereby literature is displaced in favor of linguistically unsophisticated print media and pornography is likened to the spinning of a spider's web, which is of course the device it employs to capture and immobilize its prey. Technology, according to Beatty, is to blame for the oppressive world around them. Bradbury, through Beatty, is issuing a warning—that unchecked technological development, mindless thrill-seeking in media, and the political anomie of the majority, create in American society a drastic vulnerability to a progressive degeneration of its cultural and intellectual capacities, with a corresponding decay of its democratic political institutions.

Beatty's tone then turns fatherly and admonishing; he urges Montag to be careful, and to stick to his duty. Beatty admits that most firemen are smitten at one time or another by a curiosity to read the books they are compelled to burn, but he insists this is merely an ordinary, perfectly natural aberration and that the tendency will pass in short order if ignored. He claims, perhaps mendaciously, in an attempt to draw Montag out, to have been a reader himself at one time, until he saw the light of the bonfires and reformed. Finally he makes it clear by means of gentle insinuation that, after all, when one is in the service of a strong, omnipresent institutionalized power that may reward or punish anyone under its control without constraint, enlightened self-interest is the only really necessary reason to obey.

Captain Beatty finally leaves Montag alone to make up his mind, and now comes a pivotal early moment in the novel, which will determine all the ensuing events. Now that he has come to a preliminary understanding of the nature of the tyranny whose functionary he is, he must decide whether he will accept his place as a cog in a machinery of oppression, or, in some way, offer resistance to the machine. Not knowing clearly how, except insofar as it involves reading books, Montag chooses to resist. The despotism under which he lives is made possible, was in fact created, by its own people, whom Bradbury clearly blames for their own problems, largely as a consequence of their failure to care, to reflect, and to think carefully. Caring and thinking are of greatest importance when they result in deliberate choices, and the result of a failure of caring and thinking is a kind of passive choice, imputed to the people even though they had few resources with which to choose otherwise. Thanks to his privileged position, Montag is able to take advantage of a rare opportunity to decide to care, to think, and, consequently, to read.

The first passage he reads after Beatty's remonstrating visit is a line from *Gulliver's Travels*, a satirical novel by the eighteenth-century Irish humorist, Jonathan Swift: "It is computed, that eleven thousand persons have at several times suffered death rather than submit to break their eggs at the smaller end." The reference is to a meaningless war fought between the miniature people who populate the imaginary nations of Lilliput and Blefescu, arising from their violent disagreements about how to go about breaking eggs. It is to be noted that the political system of the Lilliputians is extensively described by Swift, involving a wholly arbitrary system of appointments masquerading as a democracy.

Fahrenheit 451's second section, **The Sieve and the Sand**, follows Montag as he gropes his way toward a position of defiance. He begins with a rather ill-advised attempt to draw Mildred into the current of his new thinking, initiating this campaign by reading aloud to her. The first selection he tries comes from James Boswell's famous biography of his friend, Samuel Johnson—virtually the sole author of the first dictionary of the English language—the *Life of Johnson*: "We cannot tell the precise moment when friendship is formed. As in filling a vessel drop by drop, there is at last a drop which makes it run over; so in a series of kindnesses there is at last one which makes the heart run over." This compares favorably to the passage in which Montag's feelings for Clarisse congeal out of a number of symbolic liquids. It may be supposed therefore that he is, by virtue of this effort to awaken Mildred's mind, trying to make possible with her the same love that he felt for the late Clarisse. However, Mildred is able to relate only to a brief aside from Boswell himself, in which he adverts to: "... That favourite subject, Myself." Not only is this quotation brief enough, at four words, to appear entire and undivided in the extremely narrow aperture of her television-constricted attention span, but it appeals to her as an expression of her own relation to herself, which is precisely what makes it impossible for her to relate to her husband or to anyone else. Mildred is not exactly selfish, rather she is trapped in and overwhelmed by a self that she cannot understand and seeks only to escape, along with the rest of reality.

While she is too far gone to register the meaning of his reading, and experiences something akin to withdrawal symptoms when separated from the television for more than a brief length of time, she is also too lost in delusions to bother threatening to expose him to the other firemen. At this point, Montag remembers a visit to a public park, during which he had, by chance, happened to meet a man named Faber. This man had once been an English professor, before the universal ban on books made his occupation redundant. Drawing on his resources as a fireman, Montag contacts Faber, who, he hopes, can more lucidly and extensively explain the appeal and benefit of reading, and who would presumably be sympathetic to Montag in his new predicament. Faber reluctantly and suspiciously agrees to receive a visit from Montag in his apartment, and Montag, to prove his good faith, shows Faber a Bible he has confiscated. Beginning to trust Montag, Faber begins to open up to him. Faber says the real problem is not so much the machinery, the technological development to which Beatty attributed the new climate of intellectual and cultural sterility, as a kind of sourceless despair that causes people to turn their back on reading, on thinking, on being individuals.

> Remember, the firemen are rarely necessary. The public itself stopped reading of its own accord. You firemen provide a circus now and then at which buildings are set off and crowds gather for the pretty blaze, but it's a small sideshow indeed, and hardly necessary to keep things in line ...

> That was a year I came to class at the start of the new semester and found only one student to sign up for Drama from Aeschylus to O'Neill. You see? How like a beautiful statue of ice it was, melting in the sun. I remember the newspapers dying like huge moths. No one *wanted* them back. No one missed them. And then the Government, seeing how advantageous it was to have people reading only about passionate lips and the fist in the stomach, circled the situation with your fire-eaters.

Faber's reasoning is curious for a number of reasons. His use of the image of the moth is one that Beatty employs elsewhere in much the same context, and, for all that he was formerly a man of letters, and operates in the novel as a subversive, Faber accounts for the current state of affairs in almost exactly the same way. He agrees with Beatty that the state merely confirmed after the fact a decision that had actually already been made by the majority, such that this tyranny is one that was permitted to happen by a lazy and selfish people, who therefore deserve what they get. To a considerable extent, Faber represents the degree to which even intellectuals are compelled to adopt the party line even when they strive to critique it. Faber's position is at least partially contradictory; he says that he opposes tyranny, but this is a tyranny rooted in the tendencies of the largest proportion of the weirdly disinterested and mentally numb population. He acknowledges the power of books, the danger that they represent to the despotism of Bradbury's dystopia, and yet the censorship he describes is entirely redundant—why would the state need to censor books if no one wants to read them anyway? Plainly, Faber himself is no better able to account for the history of this tyranny than is Beatty. Both, in their own way, are just as ignorant as is Montag at the beginning of the novel, because they both lack the resources, even in Faber's case, to generate a critical history of their own circumstances. While Faber reads, he is isolated from the intellectual culture that helps to give meaning to reading, and for that matter he retains an elitism Bradbury feels is innate to the academic or scholarly approach to literature insofar as it criticizes, and does not revere, the work of literature.

Faber argues that the circulation of printed matter is tantamount to the circulation of ideas and the development of culture, and consequently should be considered essential to genuinely self-determinative democracy. His bolder, more libertarian point of view encourages Montag, who begins tentatively sketching out a scheme to ruin the fire department by planting books in the homes of the other firemen. Faber points out the scheme to plant books is hopelessly impractical, dangerous, and that it isn't calculated to produce any actual change; Montag's plan, while well-intentioned, simply is not radical enough. In fact, Faber, in addition to being an elitist, is also a fatalist; he believes that society can't be changed, it can only be destroyed. It is assumed that no one can have the self-awareness or historical knowledge adequate to strive rationally and programmatically for change, and, even were alert and self-possessed persons to appear on the scene, the inert mass of mankind is too stupid and conventional to save itself from itself. Bradbury instead suggests that the superior individuals withdraw from society and wait for it to collapse; only when a given society self-destructs, in what could be understood as a spasm of self-loathing, can the intellectuals emerge from hiding and rebuild society on a better basis, drawing on the repudiated and lost knowledge rejected by the masses. With the advent of nuclear weapons, humanity found itself confronting the prospect of destruction on an inconceivable scale, but such annihilation was not regarded as being entirely devoid of romance. For many writers, and science fiction writers in particular, notably Bradbury, such destruction also held out the promise of a correction in the course of human history. This correction would take the form of a drastic, admittedly horrific reduction in the size of the human population, and in the economic development of the productive capacities of society, consequently shrinking and slowing society to a point at which it would once again become manageable, as it is believed to have been in the past.

Still uncertain about Montag, but willing to go out on a limb, Faber gives him an earpiece radio which operates like an inaudible walkie-talkie. With this, they will be able to exchange messages in a way that will not attract attention. At this point, Faber begins to act as something like Montag's conscience, or another self. The two characters undergo a strange linkage, brought about by means of a technologically sophisticated device that creates a discursive intimacy between them.

A growing propensity to thoughtfulness appears in Montag's character, as his mind begins to work without requiring the prompting of other characters. In particular, his love for the vanished Clarisse begins to grow clearer to him.

> Montag shook his head. He looked at a blank wall. The girl's face was there, really quite beautiful in memory: astonishing in fact. She had a very thin face like the dial of a small clock seen faintly in a dark room in the middle of the night when you waken to see the time and see the clock telling you the hour and the minute and the second, with a white silence and a glowing, all

certainty and knowing what it has to tell us of the night passing swiftly on toward further darknesses, but moving also toward a new sun.

"*What?*" asked Montag of that other self, that sub-conscious idiot that ran babbling at times, quite independent of will, habit, and conscience.

Whether or not the girl is actually Clarisse in this passage matters less than that it was his encounter with her, and the sequence of events to which it helped to give rise, made possible the development of his "other self," or, at least, made it audible to him for the first time. Montag reacts with incredulity to discover these poetic words in himself. The image of the girl appears as he gazes at a blank wall, which is to say, at a wall without a television. His imagination is the living model, and the television is the simulated imagination; there is a homologous structure, for example, in the comparison of the definitively alive Clarisse with the living-dead Mildred.

He felt his smile slide away, fold over and down on itself like a tallow skin, like the stuff of a fantastic candle burning too long and now collapsing and now blown out. Darkness. He was not happy. He said the words to himself. He recognized this as the true state of affairs. He wore his happiness like a mask and the girl had run off across the lawn with the mask and there was no way of going to knock on her door and ask for it back.

In this passage, darkness returns, this time as a consequence of the melting away of a candle. Montag has already associated Clarisse in his mind with a candle, and with his mother in the same passage, so the reader should not overlook the reappearance of the candle, or "tallow," failing to realize these associations will also be involved. The girl he dares not name to himself is plainly Clarisse, who has undone the false happiness, which was only a superficial appearance, and not the true happiness that, according to Bradbury, must come from within.

Returning home, Montag discovers that his wife has also sought out reinforcements, her two friends Mrs. Bowles and Mrs. Phelps, and all three of them are basking in the respectable narcotic of the television again.

"Isn't this show wonderful?" cried Mildred.
"Wonderful!"
On one wall a woman smiled and drank orange juice simultaneously. How does she do both at once? thought Montag, insanely. In the other walls an x-ray of the same woman revealed the contracting journey of the refreshing beverage on the way to her delighted stomach! Abruptly the room took off on a rocket flight into the clouds, it plunged into a lime-green sea where blue fish ate red and yellow fish. A minute later, Three White Cartoon Clowns chopped off each other's limbs to the accompaniment of immense incoming tides of laughter. Two minutes more and the room whipped out of town to the jet cars wildly circling an arena, bashing and backing up and bashing each other again. Montag saw a number of bodies fly in the air.
"Millie, did you *see* that!"
"I saw it, I *saw* it!"
Montag reached inside the parlor wall and pulled the main switch. The images drained away, as if the water had been let from a gigantic crystal bowl of hysterical fish.

Here, greatly compressed, are all the aspects of modernity indicted by Bradbury as contributing to the spiritual decline of humanity. There is advertising, and the intrusive X-ray and infusion of orange juice recalls to the reader Mildred's grotesque revivification by the machinery which invaded her body and replaced her blood. There is velocity, the room seeming to career fantastically through space, to travel without going anywhere. The viewer is dazzled by a representation of high speeds, bright colors, exaggerated images of the natural world which replace the real thing, again not unlike Mildred's operation. There is also unreal violence, stripped of all its emotional content and reduced to mere spectacle. Mildred and her friends take all in this violence without empathy, or even the abstract understanding that they are witnessing the infliction of pain. In fact, this kind of viewing is effectively the opposite of true witnessing, as the viewer has no relationship of any kind with the image, apart from the extremely basic relationship of the stimulated to the source of stimulation.

Montag's intellectual development has gone somewhat to his head, and what's more, it is clear in this moment that all his efforts to alter Mildred's benighted idiocy and media addiction by reading with her have been fruitless. Part of the conditioning Bradbury attributes to his dystopia is the suppression of emotion, in particular of disruptive emotions that might cause discomfort in another. The highest aim of Montag's society is the unbroken comfort of its citizens. Already pressed beyond the limits of his patience, Montag allows his frustration to emerge without taking into consideration the dangers of such open rebellion. Unable to reach Mildred intellectually or sympathetically, he symbolically attacks her by shutting down the television. He intensifies his attack then by reading to his wife and her friends, who, like all good society wives, exist only to express prim disapproval and to be scandalized, notably the famous poem "Dover Beach" by Victorian poet and influential critic, Matthew Arnold.

"Ah, love, let us be true
To one another! for the world, which seems
To lie before us like a land of dreams,
So various, so beautiful, so new,
Hath really neither joy, nor love, nor light,
Nor certitude, nor peace, nor help for pain;
And we are here, as on a darkling plain
Swept with confused alarms of struggle and flight,
Where ignorant armies clash by night."

Arnold, a middle-class critic of Victorian society who demanded of culture that it cultivate the values of "sweetness and light," and referred to "faith in machinery" as a "besetting danger," is very much in Bradbury's mind throughout the novel. *Fahrenheit 451* could be called a work of Arnoldian social criticism without too much controversy. This poem takes on a bitterly ironic tone in this context, as Montag addresses, perhaps yet with an imploring note, the zombie-like Mildred as his "love" and begs her to be "true." Here he is plainly issuing to her an ultimatum to choose between the television, and by extension the entire mediascape which is the only form of socialization permitted by the state, and himself. The poem strikingly goes on to say that the glory, the beauty, the happiness, and the comfort of the civilization to which it refers is only an illusion, and that in fact society is a dark battlefield of blind and meaningless violence, not unlike the kind Mildred and her friends have been enjoying on television. Bradbury sees to it that this quotation is all the more apt in that the threat of war is forever reinforced by the state and its media, even though there is no clear reason for such a war, nor is there any sense of the identity of the enemy. Thus, in this world filled with soldiers, it is difficult to say, as on a battlefield without light, whether one side fights the other, or a single side fights in confusion against itself.

After his outburst with the two wives, Montag unhappily departs his house to answer a call to the fire house.

> On the way downtown he was so completely alone with his terrible error that he felt the necessity for the strange warmness and goodness that came from a familiar and gentle voice speaking in the night. Already, in a few short hours, it seemed that he had known Faber a lifetime. Now he knew that he was two people, that he was above all Montag, who knew nothing, who did not even know himself a fool, but only suspected it. And he knew also that he was the old man who talked to him and talked to him as the train was sucked from one end of the night city to the other one on a long sickening gasp of motion.

While his split with Mildred and her circle is now complete, and not to be repaired, Montag is not wholly alone. He is joined to Faber, who becomes, for him, possibly as a consequence of his failure to find anyone else who might qualify, the embodiment of the reverent idea of reading that Bradbury is at some pains explaining in the novel, and for that matter, a kind of living vessel of memory: specifically, a link to the bygone time when reading was still possible. It is the role of memory, particularly that of sanctified memory, to console people in times of tribulation, according to Bradbury, exactly as Faber consoles Montag in this scene.

As he feared, his conspicuously nonconformist behavior has been registered at once, and, when Montag arrives at the firehouse, Captain Beatty is already well aware of Montag's defection. He taunts Montag with snide quotations of his own, which again give rise to the question, how Beatty can know as much about literature as he does. Bradbury implies that Beatty knows literature, and nevertheless betrays it, making him not merely ignorant, as Montag had been when the novel opened, but a fanatic, who has self-consciously dedicated himself to mediocrity and imposed uniformity as the greatest public good. Montag is trapped; his life is entirely at stake, and yet he can't shake off the vision of finer things and free thinking he's encountered through his association with Clarisse and Faber. Having made this discovery, it is no longer possible for him to resume his former ignorance, unless, perhaps, the same memory-altering operation that wiped away Mildred's memory of her suicide attempt were to be employed on him. In any event, such a return would be to the life he had known prior to his awakening, which he has come to regard in the meantime as a living death. The alternative, for Montag, would be to become like Captain Beatty himself, destroying books and imposing conformity, monstrous as those acts are, of his own free will. An alarm is abruptly reported. The address is Montag's own home.

The final section of *Fahrenheit 451*, entitled **Burning Bright** (a reference to a famous if not strictly relevant poem,

"The Tyger," by William Blake), opens with the arrival of Beatty and Montag at his own home. Mildred herself has reported Montag to the authorities. Beatty is in a position to subject Montag to a de facto test of his loyalties. This passage affords us another glimpse into Beatty's character. At one point, Montag, in what is already a literary reflex, hearkens back to the earlier period of his association with Beatty.

> He could hear Beatty's voice. "Sit down, Montag. Watch. Delicately, like the petals of a flower. Light the first page, light the second page. Each becomes a black butterfly. Beautiful, eh? Light the third page from the second and so on, chain smoking, chapter by chapter, all the silly things the words mean, all the false promises, all the second-hand notions and time-worn philosophies." There sat Beatty, perspiring gently, the floor littered with swarms of black moths that had died in a single storm.

This poetic language in the service of the destruction of poetry plants the seed in Montag's mind of a possibility, that Beatty in fact loathes himself and wishes to die. This, of course, is a self-serving conclusion on Montag's part, but there is also the implication by Bradbury that the dystopian world he has created is an extension of self-destructive tendencies in the contemporary society from which it is drawn.

> He examined his eternal matchbox, the lid of which said GUARANTEED: ONE MILLION LIGHTS OF THIS LIGHTER, and began to strike the chemical match abstractedly, blow out, strike, blow out, strike, speak a few words, blow out. He looked at the flame. He blew, he looked at the smoke. "When will you be well?"

As is often the case in dystopian fiction, the powers that be find voice in a designated apologist, who utters the seductive arguments of the powerful. Another common element of dystopian fiction is the conceit, on the part of the state, that those who oppose it or are merely unhappy with it are not legitimate critics but unwell, mentally ill. Often forms of "treatment" are proposed to "cure" the malcontent, which prove to be nothing other than brainwashing or a brutal stripping away of the mind. Through Beatty, the state "medicalizes" the question of murdering its critics, not only by treating them as if they were somehow ill (a strategy which may even convince the critic him- or herself), but to treat the critic as a disease tout court, infecting and weakening the body politic of the state, represented as a single vast organism.

"What is there about fire that's so lovely? No matter what age we are, what draws us to it?" Beatty blew out the flame and lit it again. "It's perpetual motion; the thing man wanted to invent but never did. Or almost perpetual motion. If you let it go on, it'd burn our lifetimes out. What is fire? It's a mystery. Scientists give us gobbledegook about friction and molecules. But they don't really know. Its real beauty is that it destroys responsibility and consequences. A problem gets too burdensome, then into the furnace with it. Now, Montag, you're a burden. And fire will lift you off my shoulders, clean, quick, sure; nothing to rot later. Antibiotic, aesthetic, practical."

Fire is employed in extreme cases to achieve a crude form of sterilization of wounds, known as cauterizing. Beatty proposes nothing less than cauterizing, destroying Montag, as an unclean thing, an imperfection in the state. Beatty has become something like a human avatar of fire, being wholly inconsistent, and mindlessly destructive. Even after Montag has, to preserve himself, burned his own home and his cache of books, it becomes clear that Beatty will not be satisfied until Montag is himself dead, although his motives for wishing to take Montag's life are unclear. The two men batten on each other, and, while grappling, the small transmitter provided to Montag by Faber is knocked loose and falls on the ground, where Beatty finds it. Now Montag's problems are especially acute, because, in tracing the signal from the transmitter, Beatty will inevitably be led to Faber. While Montag is selfless enough to confront his own destruction by the state, he realizes, now Beatty threatens his "other self," the literary self of memory and reverence that Faber is. In order to protect Faber, Montag burns Captain Beatty alive, turning his fire back upon him.

In its relentless pursuit of printed matter, the fire department employs a Mechanical Hound, a lethal robot and control machine with special detectors enabling it to "sniff out" the presence of books as an actual bloodhound can detect and track fugitives. These Hounds are not simply tools, but terrifying monsters designed to intimidate citizens and frighten them into obedience. As a fugitive now himself, Montag has much to fear from the Mechanical Hound, but, as a former fireman, Montag is familiar with the means to deactivate the Hound, and does so.

With nothing left to lose, Montag's flight from the authorities is a simplified flight to freedom. He quickly ascertains that another Mechanical Hound is chasing him, and this chase is relayed live to the public on television, as an illustration of the futility of resistance to the state, and the impossibility of escape. Montag, however, does manage to escape, by taking to the water; specifically, to a river which bears him safely away from the Mechanical Hound, which is unable to "smell" him in the water and, for that matter, unable to enter the water itself without shorting out its electronics and becoming incapacitated. Thwarted, the state saves face by destroying another person and passing him off to the public as the fugitive. Montag himself is borne away on the current of the river to safety.

> He felt as if he had left a stage behind and many actors. He felt as if he had left the great seance and all the murmuring ghosts. He was moving from an unreality that was frightening into a reality that was unreal because it was new.

In this passage, the astute reader will note again the tendency, again perhaps self-serving, on the part of Montag to see the citizens of the state as being already dead, and no different in quality of their reality than phantom images on the television. And the state has, as far as Bradbury's dystopia is concerned, executed Montag; the entire principle of its operation is replacement of the actual with the false, and this principle obtains even to its own citizens.

Having made good his escape, Montag begins to rediscover the creatural existence his sanitized society had sought, according to Bradbury, to hide from him.

How long he stood he did not know, but there was a foolish and yet delicious sense of knowing himself as an animal come from the forest, drawn by the fire. He was a thing of brush and liquid eye, of fur and muzzle and hoof, he was a thing of horn and blood that would smell like autumn if you bled it out on the ground."

Montag is eventually drawn to the campfire of a group of wandering derelicts, or so they might seem. Many of them are former city dwellers, and, it transpires, they, like Montag, are all of them readers. They monitor events inside the city, with particular attention to the escape of fugitives and dissidents, and are not fooled by the state's executions of imposters. They were aware of Montag's flight and knew where to go to meet him, it being their practice to approach all successful runaways with the intention of recruiting them. Montag is very satisfied to join this group, whose leader, Granger, explains that they are all individually entrusted with the memorization of canonical works of western literature as a sort of living library.

... hold on to one thought: you're not important. You're not anything. Some day the load we're carrying with us may help someone. But even when we had the books on hand, a long time ago, we didn't use what we got out of them. We went right on insulting the dead. We went right on spitting on the graves of all the poor ones who died before us. We're going to meet a lot of lonely people in the next week and the next month and the next year. And when they ask us what we're doing, you can say, We're remembering. That's where we'll win out in the long run. And some day we'll remember so much that we'll build the biggest steamshovel in history and dig the biggest grave of all time and shove war in and cover it up.

Bradbury's strategy in characterizing Granger is interesting, in that he gives him the same basic perspective as was surprisingly shared by Faber and by Beatty. The individual is unimportant, as is the present, and society is to blame for its own devastation. Above all, however, Granger diverges from Beatty in the importance he places on remembering, where Beatty, and by extension all of Bradbury's dystopia, places the highest premium on forgetting. Granger goes on:

And when the war's over, some day, some year, the books can be written again, the people will be called in, one by one, to recite what they know, and we'll set it up in type until another Dark Age, when we might have to do the whole thing over again.

The gruff populism of these passages is meant to show that one like Granger can be both cultured and rugged, heroic and cerebral. His tone suggests a blunt and unromantic realism and practicality which are intended by Bradbury to give the reader an impression of hope, that the revival of society is possible where it is contained within a single, efficacious vision.

All we want to do is keep the knowledge we think we will need, intact and safe. We're not out to incite or anger anyone yet. For if we are destroyed, the knowledge is dead, perhaps for good. We are model citizens, in our own special way; we walk the old tracks, we lie in the hills at night, and the city people let us be. We're stopped and searched occasionally, but there's nothing on our persons to incriminate us. The organization is flexible, very loose, and fragmentary. Some of us have had plastic surgery on our faces and fingerprints. Right now we have a horrible job; we're waiting for the war to begin and, as quickly, end. It's not pleasant, but then we're not in control, we're the odd minority crying in the wilderness. When the war's over, perhaps we can be of some use in the world."

Note that even here, war is treated as a non-historical catastrophe and a purely technical one; Bradbury is steadily and deftly shifting the mode of the narrative toward fable, implying that what may be imagined as occurring in the future may also be conceived of as having taken place already, in the past.

As a member of the group, Montag is called upon to memorize one of the books of the Bible, Ecclesiastes, which says that all human endeavor is "vanity, and a striving after wind." As he begins to acclimatize himself to his new life, he is again reminded of Clarisse.

During the night, he thought, below the loft, he would hear a sound like feet moving, perhaps. He would tense and sit up. The sound would move away. He would lie back and look out the loft window, very late in the night, and see the lights go out in the farmhouse itself, until a very young and beautiful woman would sit in an unlit window, braiding her hair. It would be hard to see her, but her face would be like the face of the girl so long ago in his past now, so very long ago, the girl who had known the weather and never been burnt by the fireflies, the girl who had known what dandelions meant rubbed off on your chin. Then, she would be gone from the warm window and appear again upstairs in her moon-whitened room. And then, to the sound of death, the sound of the jets cutting the sky in two black pieces beyond the horizon, he would lie in the loft, hidden and safe, watching those strange new stars over the rim of the earth, fleeing from the soft color of dawn."

The fire of fireflies is entirely natural, and harmless; an image associated with love. The awesome power of the jets is contrasted to the pastoral and nostalgic simplicity of a scene whose subtext would seem to be that man is better fitted to a smaller, more contained, slower, and rural existence than to the uncontrollable technical vastness of futuristic cities. The sudden effervescence of the jets suggests that human technological accomplishment is a fleeting thing in more ways than one, when compared with the stately immutability of the stars.

From their pastoral refuge, the nomad bibliophiles are able to look on in safety as the novel's deus ex machina, a nightmarish war involving high-tech, city-demolishing weapons, intervenes. A nameless, remote enemy, engaged in a long-standing and meaningless war with the state Montag once served, completely destroys the city from afar. The book ends in a mood of chastened optimism not uncommon in Bradbury's work, with the prospect of enduring resistance to conformity and the ultimately reassuring idea that even the very functionaries of oppression, such as Montag had been, are not beyond conversion to a more liberated point of view. Granger delivers a sermon on the Phoenix, which rises from the ashes of its own immolation to a new immortality, also brought about by fire, to illustrate his plan to build a new society, and to restore the canonical texts of old from the memories of the nomads.

Critical Views

PETER SISARIOS ON LITERARY AND BIBLICAL ALLUSIONS

But if we look more closely at the novel, noting specifically the literary and Biblical allusions, we see a deeper message in the novel than simply the warning that our society is headed for intellectual stagnation. The literary allusions are used to underscore the emptiness of the twenty-fourth century, and the Biblical allusions point subtly toward a solution to help us out of our intellectual "Dark Age." Bradbury seems to be saying that the nature of life is cyclical and we are currently at the bottom of an intellectual cycle. We must have faith and blindly hope for an upward swing of the cycle. This concept of the natural cycle is most explicitly stated by Bradbury through the character of Granger:

> And when the war's over, some day, some year, the books can be written again, the people will be called in, one by one, to recite what they know, and we'll set it up in type until another Dark Age, when we might have to do the whole thing over again.

The major metaphor in the novel, which supports the idea of the natural cycle, is the allusion to the Phoenix, the mythical bird of ancient Egypt that periodically burned itself to death and resurrected from its own ashes to a restored youth. Through the persona of Granger, Bradbury expresses the hope that mankind might use his intellect and his knowledge of his own intellectual and physical destruction to keep from going through endless cycles of disintegration and rebirth.

This image of the Phoenix is used in the novel in association with the minor character Captain Beatty, Montag's superior. As an officer, Beatty has knowledge of what civilization was like before the contemporary society of the novel. In an attempt to satisfy Guy's curiosity and hopefully to quell any further questioning, Beatty relates to Guy how the twentieth century began to decline intellectually, slowly reaching the point in future centuries of banning books, schools stopped teaching students to think or to question and crammed them with factual data in lieu of an education. Psychological hedonism became the most positive virtue; all questioners and thinkers were eliminated. It is crucial that Beatty wears the sign of the Phoenix on his hat and rides in a "Phoenix car." He has great knowledge of the past yet ironically and tragically does not know how to use his knowledge, treating it only as historical curiosity. He is interested only in keeping that status quo of uninterrupted happiness and freedom from worry. He imparts his knowledge only to firemen who are going through the inevitable questioning he feels all firemen experience. He tells Guy that fiction only depicts an imaginary world, and all great ideas are controversial and debatable; books then are too indefinite. Appropriately, Beatty is burned to death, and his death by fire symbolically illustrates the rebirth that is associated with his Phoenix sign. When Guy kills Beatty, he is forced to run off and joins Granger; this action is for Guy a rebirth to a new intellectual life.

Bradbury employs several specific literary quotations to illustrate the shallowness of Guy's world. By using references to literature, Bradbury carries through a basic irony in the book: he is using books to underscore his ideas about a world in which great books themselves have been banned.

After Beatty has given Guy a capsule history of how the world reached the anti-intellectual depths of the twenty-fourth century, Guy goes to a book he has concealed but has not yet had the courage to read. He reads several pages; then Bradbury has him quote the following passage:

> It is computed, that eleven thousand persons have at several times suffered death rather than submit to break their eggs at the smaller end.

The quotation is from the first book of Swift's *Gulliver's Travels*, "A Voyage to Lilliput." At that point of the quotation

Gulliver has learned of a long-standing feud in Lilliput, between those who have traditionally broken their eggs at the larger end, and the edict of the King, ordering all subjects to break their eggs at the smaller end because a member of the royal family had once cut his finger breaking the larger end. The struggle between being reasonable and being saddled to tradition even to the point of ridiculous suicide is perhaps what Bradbury is after here. The twenty-fourth century is just as saddled to the status quo, and Bradbury has been careful to point out the dangers of intellectual deadness. The example from Lilliput is an excellent one for him to choose, since it represents an absurd situation taken to a gross exaggeration, a basic device of satire.

As Guy and his wife read on, a quotation is taken directly from Boswell's *Life of Johnson:*

> We cannot tell the precise moment when friendship is formed. As in filling a vessel drop by drop there is at last a drop which makes it run over; so in a series of kindnesses there is at last one which makes the heart run over.

Guy makes the point that this quote brings to his mind the girl next door, Clarisse McClennan, who was labeled a "time bomb" by Beatty because she was a sensitive, observant person who questioned society, and was consequently eliminated by the government. Montag made an emotional attachment to Clarisse, an attachment that was sincere and true in a world hostile to honesty. It was his relationship with Clarisse that was for Guy the first "drop"; she started his questioning of the status quo, and subsequent events after her death made Guy think and question more and more seriously, until he completely breaks away from his diseased society at the end of the novel.

Guy continues to read and quotes again from Boswell, this time from a letter to Temple in 1763: "That favourite subject, Myself." Curiously enough, Guy's wife Mildred, who has not received any inspiration from this secret reading session, says that she understands this particular quote. Her statement is juxtaposed against Guy's saying that Clarisse's favorite subject wasn't herself, but others. He realizes the truth of the statements he has been reading from authors who wrote hundreds of years ago; his wife can only understand the literal level of one statement, the one reflecting the self-interest of her society.

The only other direct quote Bradbury employs from literature comes in the second part of the book, and serves to underscore the emptiness of the world that the three preceding quotes have shown. After Guy returns from having visited Faber, he talks with his wife and two of her friends. The conversation of the women reflects the shallowness of the women's thinking, since they are the products of this empty culture. Their discussion of politics, for example, has to do with voting for a candidate for president because he was better looking than his opponent. Guy has a book of poetry with him, and Mildred's visitors are shocked that he has a book. In a scene reminiscent of the banquet in *Macbeth*, Guy's wife attempts to cover for him by telling the women that firemen are allowed to bring books home occasionally to show their families how silly books are. Guy reads from Matthew Arnold's "Dover Beach"; the last two stanzas are quoted, and the last one is particularly apt, since it shows two lovers looking at what appears to be a happy world, but recognizing the essential emptiness that exists:

> Ah, love, let us be true
> To one another! For the world, which seems
> To lie before us like a land of dreams
> So various, so beautiful, so new,
> Hath really neither joy, nor love, nor light,
> Nor certitude, nor peace, nor help for pain;
> And we are here, as on a darkling plain
> Swept with confused alarms of struggle and flight,
> Where ignorant armies clash by night.

Guy's world, too, rests on happiness, a happiness of psychological comfort and freedom from controversy, but Guy is finding that beneath the exterior is a vast emptiness, a "darkling plain."

Thus far, we have seen how Bradbury has used several allusions to literature to describe the situation of the contemporary world of the novel. It might be wise at this point to note an historical reference made, one that serves to underscore some basic ideas in the book.

Early in the book, when Guy is first beginning to undergo doubts, he and his squad are called to the home of a woman discovered owning books. The woman refuses to leave her home, choosing to die in the flames with her books. On the way back to the firehouse, Guy, shaken by the experience, mentions to Beatty the last words of the woman, "Master Ridley." Beatty—and note again that he has the knowledge—tells Guy that the woman was referring to Nicholas Ridley, Bishop of London in the sixteenth century, who was arrested as a heretic because he allowed dissenters to speak freely. He was burned at the stake with fellow heretic Hugh Latimer, who spoke the words to Ridley that the woman in the novel alludes to as her last words: "We shall this day light such a candle, by God's grace, in England, as I trust shall never be put out." These words recall the Phoenix idea of rebirth by fire, since the woman's death proves to be an important factor in Guy's decision to investigate books. The words are ironic in the sense that the intellectual candle in Montag's world is burning rather dimly at the time, but the words are at the same time a fine statement of the indestructibility of questioners and thinkers in any society.

There are four specific Biblical allusions in the novel, and an examination of them shows that they both support the idea of the natural cycle and contribute to Bradbury's solution to helping us out of, or rather avoiding, the type of world pictured by the literary allusions. This solution would be the natural philosophical outlook that would be held by those who believe in a natural cycle to life and are in the midst of the bottom of a cycle: one must wait and have faith, since things will eventually improve.

Two of the Biblical allusions that support the idea of a philosophical faith in the renewal of cycles are the references to the Lilies of the Field (Matthew 6:28) and to the book of Job. Saint Matthew's parable of the Lilies illustrates that God takes care of all things and we need not worry; the Lilies don't work or worry, yet God provides for them. This submission to faith, this feeling that God will provide all in due course is also affirmed by the reference to the Book of Job, one of the strongest statements of faith in the face of adversity in Western culture. Both of these references come at significant points in the novel. The allusion to the Lilies of the Field comes as Guy is on his way to see Professor Faber. The Lilies are juxtaposed in zeugma-like style with Denham's Dentifrice, an advertisement Guy sees on the subway train. Both flash through his head and form an excellent contrast: the faith and submission of the Lilies and the artificiality and concern with facades of the contemporary advertisement jingle. After his clandestine meeting with Faber, at which the professor agrees to help Guy learn about books and plan for the future, Guy gets a message from Faber through the small earplug he wears to keep in contact with the teacher. The message simply says, "The Book of Job," in a sense reminding Guy that he must have faith, for the going will be rough on his new venture.

Two other Biblical allusions come at the end of the novel, when Guy has joined Granger and his colleagues. This group of men memorizes great works of our culture as a means of preserving ideas until literature is once again permitted. Guy is assigned to read and memorize the Book of Ecclesiastes, the Old Testament book that asserts the need to submit to the natural order of things. The only direct quotation from Ecclesiastes comes from Chapter Three, the well-known chapter that echoes the natural cycle idea in its opening line, "To everything there is a season…" The line comes to Guy as the men trudge along in Canterbury-like procession away from the destroyed city, each man being required to recite aloud from his assigned work in order to bolster their spirit and comradeship. Guy thinks first of some phrases from Ecclesiastes, appropriately enough, "A time to break down, and a time to build up," and "A time to keep silence and a time to speak." Another quote then comes to Guy, this one from the

Book of Revelations, which Guy had told Granger he partially remembered:

> And on either side of the river was there a tree of life which bore twelve manner of fruits, and yielded her fruit every month; and the leaves of the tree were for the healing of nations (22:2).

This last book of the New Testament, also known as the Book of the Apocalypse, tells us that a victory of God is certain, but that much struggle must come first; we must have faith and endure before we can enjoy the fruits of victory. The lines Bradbury has Guy recall not only reinforce the idea of a cyclical world, but also give us a key to Bradbury's hope that "the healing of nations" can best come about through a rebirth of man's intellect. We must use our minds to halt the endless cycles of destruction by warfare and rebirth to a world of uneasy peace and intellectual death. The twelve tribes of Israel wandering in the desert seeking a new nation can be recalled here as Montag, Granger, and the others wander away from the city with hope that their new world will soon be established.

WAYNE L. JOHNSON ON THEMES IN THE NOVEL

Fahrenheit 451 is one of only two novels that Bradbury has written. The other is *Something Wicked This Way Comes*. (*Dandelion Wine* and *The Martian Chronicles* are often referred to as novels but they are really collections of separate stories unified by theme and specially written bridge passages.) *Fahrenheit 451* is a short novel, an expansion of a story, "The Fireman," originally published in *Galaxy*. The book is about as far as Bradbury has come in the direction of using science fiction for social criticism. Actually, the premise of the book is rather farfetched—that firemen in some future state no longer fight fires but set them, having become arms of a political program aimed at stamping out all literature. This purging of the written word, particularly of the imaginative sort, is found in other stories, most strikingly in "Pillar of Fire" and "The Exiles." But in these other stories the tone is clearly that of a fantasy. *Fahrenheit 451* is realistic in tone, but keeps such a tight focus on the developing awareness of fireman Guy Montag that we can successfully overlook the improbability of his occupation. In fact, the very improbability of Montag's work allows Bradbury to maintain a certain detachment in the book, so that basic themes such as freedom of speech, the value of imagination, the authority of the state, individualism versus conformity, and so on, can be developed and explored without becoming either too realistic or too allegorical.

In the course of the book, Montag goes through what today might be called consciousness raising. He begins as a loyal fireman, burning what he is told to burn, progresses through a period of doubts and questioning, and ends up rebelling against the system and doing his part to keep man's literary heritage alive. But the bones of the plot do little to convey the feeling of the book. Bradbury's world here seems much closer to the present than the future—not so much in terms of its overall structure as in terms of its more intimate details. Some of the characterizations—Montag's wife, given over to drugs and mindless television; Clarisse, an archetypal hippie or flower child; and the old woman, who defies the firemen by pouring kerosene over her books and her own body before striking a match—might have been drawn from the turbulent political events of the sixties. It is almost necessary to remind oneself that *Fahrenheit 451* was published in 1953.

Many of Bradbury's pet themes are to be found in the novel. Metamorphosis is a major theme of the story, for in the course of it Montag changes from book-burner to living-book. Montag the fireman is intensely aware of the power of fire: "It was a special pleasure to see things eaten, to see things blackened and *changed*." He himself is changed every time he goes out on a job: "He knew that when he turned to the firehouse, he might wink at himself, a minstrel man, burnt-corked, in the mirror."

Machines are of crucial importance. Overall the book traces Montag's flight from the dangerous mechanical world of the city to the traditional haven of the country. Montag at first feels comfortable with machines, especially his flame-throwing equipment. The first time Montag meets Clarisse he views the scene in mechanical terms: "The autumn leaves blew over the moonlit pavement in such a way as to make the girl who was moving there seem fixed to a gliding walk, letting the motion of the wind and leaves carry her forward." But many mechanical things are repellent to Montag, particularly the equipment the medical technicians use on his wife after she has taken an overdose of sleeping pills: "They had two machines, really. One of them slid down your stomach like a black cobra down an echoing well looking for all the old water and the old time gathered there."

Montag's particular mechanical enemy is the fire station's Mechanical Hound, more like a huge spider, actually, with its "bits of ruby glass and … sensitive capillary hairs in the Nylon-brushed nostrils…that quivered gently, gently, its eight legs spidered under it on rubber-padded paws." As Montag becomes more fascinated with books and nearer to betrayal of his duties as a fireman, the hound becomes more suspicious of him. The hound is then symbolic of the relentless, heartless pursuit of the State.

When Montag finally flees the city, he must first cross a mechanical moat, a highway 100 yards across on which the "beetle" cars seem to take pleasure in using pedestrians for target practice. Other machines Montag grows to hate are the radio and television that reduce their audience, Montag's wife, for one, into listless zombies.

But *Fahrenheit 451* is not primarily a work of social criticism. Its antimachine and antiwar elements are there primarily as background for Montag's spiritual development. It is interesting that this development seems to be in the direction of social outcast. Granted that Montag's society has its evils, but at the end of the book we are not so sure that Montag will be completely happy with his new-found friends, the book people. What we are sure of is that Montag has entrenched himself as nay-sayer to a society that has become hostile and destructive toward the past. Montag joins the book people whose task, as Granger puts it, is "remembering." But even as he does so, he promises himself that he will one day follow the refugees from the bombed-out city, seeking, though this is not stated, perhaps his wife, perhaps Clarisse. Most of the book people are like the old man in "To the Chicago Abyss," essentially harmless, using their talents for remembering things to aid their society in whatever way they can. But Montag may perhaps be too rigid an idealist, having rejected his former society with the same vehemence as he once embraced it. Like Spender, but like many of Bradbury's other outsiders and misfits, Montag has successfully achieved a truce or stalemate with a world hostile to his individuality. At the end of Fahrenheit 451, Montag's future can go either way: toward reintegration with a new, less hostile society, or toward a continuing, perpetual alienation.

WILLIAM F. TOUPONCE ON REVERIE

Beyond this modicum of expectation, we should refrain at the outset from imposing any abstract generic schemes on our reading of *Fahrenheit 451*, for those critics who have not done so have been led by their preconceptions to derive false interpretations from a true response. A good case in point is John Huntington's recent study of utopian and anti-utopian logic in the novel. Huntington claims that the novel moves from dystopia to utopia, from negative to positive without evoking any critical positions in between, and he thinks that this is a deep structural contradiction which cannot be mediated except in a "blurred" fashion (imagery and evocation rather than true thought): "The dystopian and utopian possibilities in the novel are thus represented by separate clusters of images that the novel finds unambiguous and leaves unchallenged."[3] Indeed, in this view of the text, mediation produces horror rather than thought. Nature is good and technology is bad, but the ultimate horror is a mixture of the two, the mechanical hound, which combines the relentlessness of the bloodhound with the infallibility of technology.

But if both possibilities depend on systems of imagery that ignore contradictions, Huntington goes on to note the very presence of the contradiction in the novel's central symbol:

> The interesting difficulty is where do books fit into this simple opposition? Since Gutenberg the book has been a symbol of technological progress. Bradbury counters this meaning of his symbol by reducing his pastoral, not to paper books, but to humans who remember books. Thus the replication and general availability that are books' virtues, but which the novel has seen as the instruments of the mass-culture that has ruined the world, are denied. We have the idea of the book without the fact of its production. Then, by becoming a general symbol of the past now denied, the book becomes a symbol for all old values, but his symbolism brings up two difficulties. First, whatever good books have propagated, they have also preached the evils that have oppressed the world. The very technology that the novel finds threatening would be impossible without books. Second, books can readily inspire a repressive and tradition-bound pedantry which, while anti-technological, is also against nature.[4]

One wonders how Huntington could have arrived at this awareness of contradictions if the novel in fact so studiously avoids them. Thus Huntington is confused by the end of the novel where he sees the moral vision of the novel and its ideal of radiant literacy made subject to a "titanic revision of values." But to read it this way would be to suppose that Bradbury is attempting anti-utopian thought, which he admits seems unlikely. These difficulties are the result of genre theory, narrowly conceived. If Huntington had remained true to his actual experience of reading, instead of trying to impose an abstract scheme on it, he would have been led to discover the complex dialectical process by which the social criticism of the novel is effected and to a clearer perception of its themes. On the generic level, mediations are everywhere suggested, and as we will show later they evoke anything but horror.

The reader's search for the meaning and significance of utopia is in essence the subject of the book, as should be obvious from the fact that the protagonist, Montag the fireman, is caught up as a reader himself in the very contradictions Huntington mentions. This is what makes the book's portrayed world so dramatic and easily realized (quite apart from the fact that fire itself easily and dramatically brings about the phenomena of a fantastic world). Its main hypothesis—that technology, mass culture, and minority pressure brought about the world we see portrayed in the novel—is indeed made concrete for the reader *because* of the very contradictions of books. I do not mean that *Fahrenheit 451* is contradictory in the sense that it refutes its own hypothesis, but only that it does not deny the negative and contradictory values of books themselves. Why this negative value needs to be preserved is something we can now elaborate on.

Fahrenheit 451 makes vivid for the reader the whole problematic course of Western enlightenment that culminated in technology and the positivistic processes of thought its world-wide dominance have brought about. In order to know nature objectively we in a sense misrecognize or forget ourselves as part of nature. The price of progress is brought about by a kind of oblivion, like that of a surgical operation on our bodies during which we were unconscious or anesthetized. Consciousness once more restored, we find it difficult to bridge the gap between our present and our past: "The loss of memory is a transcendental condition for science. All objectification is a forgetting."[5] The disenchantment of nature and myth brings about a certain triumph of man over his fears, but by defining man in opposition to nature it sets up a program for domination and so reverts to barbarism and mythic repetition. Thus like the phoenix symbol used in the novel, history in *Fahrenheit 451* appears to go in cycles. The irony seems to be that the capacity to know and represent the world to ourselves is the measure of our domination of it, but domination—power and knowledge—are the things most often represented. Language itself (as that of Fire Chief Beatty in the novel) is used deceitfully as a tool for domination: "The capacity of representation is the vehicle of progress and regression at the same time."[6]

It is understandable then that this dialectical process is represented in *Fahrenheit 451* as a fantastic reversal of the real world. Firemen who should control fires (perhaps the ultimate symbol of technology in the novel) are lighting them instead. The reader is at first surprised by this when the novel opens immediately with a scene of house burning or arson in which Montag takes pleasure in burning books, and it sets him off on his quest for understanding the relationship between his fantastic world and his own. It is also therefore a contradiction within the imagery system of the dystopian world itself, for how can the technological world be represented by natural imagery? It seems that we must find a non-alienating way to represent the demands of unrecognized nature. Fire in this world can only be ironic enlightenment.

The principles of this false enlightenment are made apparent to the reader by the book's vitriolic attack on mass culture, which turns out to be a permanent denial of pleasure despite the power it displays and promises. No modern utopian novel insists more than *Fahrenheit 451* on the nonidentity of culture and society. The book struggles at every point to double or split the reader's forced and false identification with the society which has nurtured him. It compels the reader to discover for himself the passivity of the subject in mass culture, his loss of critical autonomy and freedom, and the general decline of negative critical forces in society—forces which could lead to a critique of existing conditions if not to utopia. This splitting constantly happens to Montag in his reading and is dramatized especially in the second part of the novel. It is here that the book registers a deeply felt fear that mass culture is threatening to collapse art as an autonomous realm of utopian freedom into the mere mechanical reproduction and repetition of the economic base. Why are books banned in this society? The reader discovers with Montag that they are the only thing left which harbors the forces of negation or principles through which the world around us could be made to appear false and alienating (what the implied author obviously thinks is the case). As the utopian wise man Faber says, books show the pores in the face of life, its gaps and discontinuities.

But what role does reverie have in the novel? This only emerges clearly in the third part of the novel when Montag has escaped the city. The third part of Bradbury's hypothesis is realized here. It was minority pressure which combined with the other two forces which eventually led to the need for everyone to be the same—to narcissism, in short. People must be mirror images of each other which means that they never have any real contact with a world outside themselves. And advertising and other media techniques are bent on artificially stimulating the consumption of grandiose images of the self within the city itself. This psychological theme is very prominent in *Fahrenheit 451*, and it is surprising that no critic has made much of it since Kingsley Amis twenty years ago.

Amis argued that the lesson to be drawn from *Fahrenheit 451* is not only that a society could be devised that would frustrate active virtues, nor even that these could eventually be suppressed, but that there is in all kinds of people something that longs for this to happen. This need presupposes not some kind of overt political action (indeed, no violent military takeover or class struggle is indicated in the novel), but a tendency in human behavior that could be reinforced if certain tendencies presently at work in society were not corrected or mitigated. Analyzing a scene from *Fahrenheit 451* in which Mildred, Montag's wife, is near suicide from a drug overdose and is listening only to the noise of an electronic Seashell, he concludes that it demonstrates to him a "fear of pleasure so overmastering that it can break down in the sense of reality or at least the pattern of active life, and break them down in everyone not merely in the predisposed neurotic."[7] Now, it is the experience of reverie in the third part of the novel which connects us to a real natural world (an Arcadian utopia, in fact) outside the narcissism of the city. The reader rediscovers through a long water-reverie, which is the exact opposite of

Mildred's, the archetypes of utopian satisfaction. We experience with Montag a non-alienating relationship to nature, and this experience of the imaginary, of another world not based on domination, enables us to effect an oneiric criticism of technological society.

It is Bradbury's strategy to link initially the experience of reverie and world with Clarisse, Montag's teenage neighbor. Montag knows that all books that are works of art are connected with her in some way, for she awakens in him the desire to read (to create an imaginary world). But we must also be given some distance from this experience of the imaginary if we are to effect social criticism. To identify completely with a character in a novel or a play, as Madame Bovary and Don Quixote do, to become the book, is romantic madness and Faber tells Montag so in the book's central section. This sort of narcissism is resisted early in the book; the reader is repeatedly split, and we should therefore not be surprised at the end when Granger, the leader of the book people, tells Montag that he is not important, but the book he remembers is. Books must preserve their independent, autonomous and negative character if they are to aid us in transforming basic impulses in the personality such as narcissism. Works of art, therefore, by representing deprivation as negative retract, as it were, the prostitution of the utopian impulse by the culture industry and rescue by mediation what was denied: "The secret of aesthetic sublimation is its representation of fulfillment as a broken promise. The culture industry does not sublimate; it represses."[8] In Bradbury's novel media are not mediations unless they have some historical content to transform in the first place. Books are the repositories of that content, the novel's utopian past.

So Bradbury's novel is itself negative in representing utopia as a broken promise and pessimistic to the extent that utopian alternatives seem to be preserved nowhere else than in the damaged lives of cultural outsiders. Yet it must be that Bradbury believes that social freedom is inseparable from enlightened thought, from remembering the mistakes of the past and not from forgetting them, because he holds out the promise that after this new Dark Age man may begin again. At the end of *Fahrenheit 451* books are no longer symbols of technological progress—of power and knowledge—but rather of wisdom.

Notes

3. Tzvetan Todorov, *The Fantastic*, trans. Richard Howard (Ithaca: Cornell University Press, 1975), p. 82.

4. Eric S Rabkin, *The Fantastic in Literature* (Princeton: Princeton University Press, 1976) p. 164.

5. W. R. Irwin, *The Game of the Impossible* (Urbana: University of Illinois Press, 1976) p. 9.

6. Darkot Suvin, *Metamorphoses of Science Fiction* (New Haven: Yale University Press, 1979) p. 68.

7. Eric S. Rabkin, *A Reader's Guide to Arthur C. Clarke* (Mercer Island: Starmont House, 1979) p. 28.

8. George Lukacs, *Writer and Critic*, trans. Arthur D. Kahn (New York: Grossel and Dunlap, 1970).

DAVID MOGEN ON *FAHRENHEIT 451* AS SOCIAL CRITICISM

If *The Martian Chronicles* (1950) established Bradbury's mainstream reputation as America's foremost science-fiction writer, publication of *Fahrenheit 451* three years later (1953) confirmed the promise of the earlier book. Indeed, these two science-fiction novels from the early fifties seem destined to survive as Bradbury's best-known and most lyrical treatment of science-fiction conventions. *The Martian Chronicles* presents the pioneering space romance in a distinctive tone of poignant irony and elegy; *Fahrenheit 451* counterpoises this ironic other-worldly drama with a searing vision of earthbound entrapment, evoking a painfully ambivalent poetry of incineration and illumination from the conventions of antiutopian fiction. Whereas *The Martian Chronicles* portrays entrapment in memory, the difficulty of accepting and adapting to an alien environment, *Fahrenheit 451* dramatizes entrapment in a sterile and poisonous culture cut off from its cultural heritage and imaginative life, vigilantly preserving a barren present without past or future. Though *Fahrenheit 451* has been accused of vagueness and sentimentality, it remains one of the most eloquent science-fiction satires, a vivid warning about mistaking, in Orville Prescott's phrase, "mindless happiness and slavish social conformity" for "progress."

Fahrenheit 451 fuses traditional themes of antiutopian fiction to focus satirically on the oppressive effect of a reductionist philosophy of "realism" translated into social policy. A very American satire, written in response to the cold war atmosphere after World War II, the novel's sarcasm is directed not at specific government institutions but at antiintellectualism and cramped materialism posing as social philosophy, justifying book burning in the service of a degraded democratic idea. *Fahrenheit 451* depicts a world in which the American Dream has turned nightmare because it has been superficially understood. For all his burning eloquence Captain Beatty represents Bradbury's satirical target, not Big Brother but the potentially tyrannical small-mindedness of the common man, perverting the most basic community institutions to enforce conformity. The underground scholar Faber warns Montag that the captain's rhetoric, like the seductive brilliance of fire, destroys the foundations of true freedom in its leveling blaze: "Remember that the Captain belongs to the most dangerous enemy to truth and freedom, the solid unmoving cattle of the majority. Oh, the terrible tyranny of the majority."

Given this satirical target—the debased Americanism of McCarthyism—the ironically reversed role of the "firemen" serves admirably as Bradbury's central metaphor, since it represents both the charismatic seductiveness of demagoguery and a perversion of the community values of Green Town, Bradbury's symbol of the American tradition at its best. Indeed, the power of *Fahrenheit 451's* imagery derives from this ironic inversion of values in an institution that once evoked Bradbury's boyish awe and respect. Writing of the personal memories that inform the novel, he recalls how like many boys he idolized local firemen prepared to battle the "bright-monster" of fire.

And I did pass the firehouse often, coming and going to the library, nights and days, in Illinois, as a boy, and I find among my notes many pages written to describe the red trucks and coiled hoses and clump-footed firemen, and I recall that night when I heard a scream from a part of my grandmother's house and ran to a room and threw open a door to look in and cry out myself.

For there, climbing on the wall, was a bright monster. It grew before my eyes. It made a great roaring sound and seemed fantastically alive as it ate of the wallpaper and devoured the ceiling.

In his memory, the firehouse is the protector of library and home. And this heroic image of the community firehouse, the curiously thrilling terror of fire, inspire the angry lyricism of Bradbury's vision of the American Dream gone awry: for in this appalling future the community firehouse has become the impersonal agent of fire itself, destroying rather than preserving the community institutions Bradbury cherishes above all others—family life, schools, and, most fundamentally of all, perhaps, the local library. As Donald Watt demonstrates in "Burning Bright: *Fahrenheit 451* as Symbolic Dystopia," ambivalent associations with fire, both destroyer and center of hearth and home, fundamentally structure the novel. But the ambivalence evoked by fire metaphorically represents the ambivalent implication of American democracy, the possibility that the communal spirit of Green Town could become an American form of totalitarianism, a "tyranny of the majority" as fearful as the tyranny of Big Brother, founded on shallow misunderstanding of rationality, science, and the nature of "happiness."

Yet if *Fahrenheit 451* gains power and specificity from its American frame of reference, the satire also applies to patterns that can recur in all societies, whenever reductionist philosophies result in the sacrifice of individuals and free play of imagination for the common good. Bradbury's satire is directed not at American ideals but at simplistic perversions of them, as well as at the American innocence that assumes totalitarianism can't happen here. However, horror at Hitler inspired the book's original conception, that to burn books is to burn people: "When Hitler burned a book I felt it as keenly, please forgive me, as burning a human, for in the long sum of history they are one and the same flesh." And though Hitler is defeated, and McCarthy's era finished, they will always have successors who will keep the firemen at work: "For while Senator McCarthy has been long dead, the Red Guard in China comes alive and idols are smashed and books are thrown to the furnace all over again. So it will go, one generation printing, another generation burning, yet another remembering what is good to remember so as to print again. Ultimately, *Fahrenheit 451* warns that tyranny and thought control always come under the guise of fulfilling ideals, whether they be those of Fascism, Communism, or the American Dream. Yet the cyclical pattern Bradbury describes also suggests the positive implications of one of the book's central symbols, the Phoenix: for like the Phoenix, mankind always arises from ashes to rediscover and refashion a desecrated cultural heritage.

Though *Fahrenheit 451* has been compared frequently to Orwell's *Nineteen Eighty-four*—an obviously influential model— it actually combines the oppressive atmosphere of Orwell's police state with a cultural milieu delivered from the other major model in the science-fiction antiutopian tradition, Huxley's *Brave New World*. Indeed, the novel's affinities with *Brave New World* are profound, since they established the basic thrust of Bradbury's satire, which is not directed at authoritarianism but at a more characteristically American problem, a reductionist, materialist image of human nature and human culture reinforced through mass entertainment media. Though the novel's basic mechanics of thought control derive from Orwell, Bradbury's satirical vision does not focus primarily on government itself but on the potentially poisonous superficiality of mass culture, on whose behalf the firemen work. As in Huxley's satire (itself profoundly influenced by American culture in the twenties), the power of totalitarianism in *Fahrenheit 451* derives primarily from pleasure rather than pain, from addiction to mindless sensation rather than from fear of government oppression. The firemen work for the "people," not for an established hierarchy. Indeed, compared to Big Brother the firemen are haphazard and mild agents of repression.

Next to Orwell's vision of totalitarianism, Bradbury's appears vaguely defined, both ideologically and politically. Montag's entrapment generates nothing like the weight of despair that crushes Winston Smith's spirit. Yet understanding the American context in which Bradbury writes clarifies the logic of this political vagueness, since his major satirical target is the leveling impulse of mass culture, rather than the rigidity of ideology. As Kingsley Amis suggests, Bradbury's style is very different from Orwell's, working through key symbols rather than through elaborately imagined detail. Yet the final effect is similarly impressive: "The book [*Fahrenheit 451*] emerges quite creditably from a comparison with *Nineteen Eighty-four* as inferior in power, but superior in conciseness and objectivity."

KEVIN HOSKINSON ON *FAHRENHEIT 451* AS A COLD WAR NOVEL

Fahrenheit 451 resumes the examination of precarious existence in an atomic age that Bradbury began in *The Martian Chronicles*. Fire as the omnipotent weapon in *Fahrenheit* finds metaphoric parallels in the notion of the bomb as the omnipotent force in the cold war years. The early tests of the Los Alamos project, for example, paid close attention to the extreme temperatures produced by the fissioning and fusioning of critical elements. J. Robert Oppenheimer, Niels Bohr, and Edward Teller based key decisions in the atomic bomb (and later the hydrogen bomb) designs on the core temperatures created at the moment of detonation. Montag and the Firemen of America, likewise, are very conscious of the key numeral 451 (the temperature at which books burn), so much so that it is printed on their helmets. The linking of hubris with the attainment of power is evident in both the Los Alamos scientists and the Firemen as well. As the Manhattan Project was drawing to a close, the team of physicists who designed the bomb came to exude a high degree of pride in their mastery of science, but without an attendant sense of responsibility. As Lamont explains, the bomb "represented the climax of an intriguing intellectual match between the scientists and the cosmos. The prospect of solving the bomb's cosmic mysteries, of having their calculations proved correct, seemed far more fascinating and important to the scientists than the prospect of their opening an era obsessed by fear and devoted to the control of those very mysteries." *Fahrenheit 451* opens with Montag similarly blinded by his own perceived importance: "He knew that when he returned to the firehouse, he might wink at himself, a minstrel man, burnt-corked, in the mirror. Later, going to sleep, he would feel the fiery smile still gripped by his face muscles, in the dark. It never went away, that smile, it never ever went away as long as he remembered." Like the engineers of atomic destruction, the engineer of intellectual destruction feels the successful completion of his goals entitles him to a legitimate smugness. The work of the cold war physicists, in retrospect, also shares something else with Montag, which Donald Watt points out: "Montag's destructive burning ... is blackening, not enlightening; and it poses a threat to nature."

Fahrenheit 451 also expands on the anxiety over the atomic bomb and fear of a nuclear apocalypse introduced in *Chronicles*. In *Fahrenheit*, Beatty endorses the official government position that, as "custodians of our peace of mind," he and Montag should "let [man] forget there is such a thing as war." Once Montag has decided to turn his back on the firehouse, however, he tries conveying his personal sense of outrage to Mildred at being kept ignorant, hoping to incite a similar concern in her: "How in hell did those bombers get up there every single second of our lives! Why doesn't someone want to talk about it! We've started and won two atomic wars since 1990!" Mildred, however, is perfectly uninspired and breaks off the conversation to wait for the White Clown to enter the TV screen. But

Montag's unheeded warning becomes reality; the bombs are dropped once Montag meets up with Granger and the book people, just as they became reality in "There Will Come Soft Rains," and Montag's horrific vision of the bomb's shock wave hitting the building where he imagines Mildred is staying captures a chilling image of his ignorant wife's last instant of life:

> Montag, falling flat, going down, saw or felt, or imagined he saw or felt the walls go dark in Millie's face, heard her screaming, because in the millionth part of time left, she saw her own face reflected there, in a mirror instead of a crystal ball, and it was such a wild empty face, all by itself in the room, touching nothing, starved and eating of itself, that at last she recognized it as her own and looked quickly up at the ceiling as it and the entire structure of the hotel blasted down upon her, carrying her with a million pounds of brick, metal, plaster and wood, to meet other people in the hives below, all on their quick way down to the cellar where the explosion rid itself of them in its own unreasonable way.

Perhaps Bradbury's own sense of fear at a future that must accommodate atomic weapons had intensified between *The Martian Chronicle*'s publication in 1950 and *Fahrenheit 451*'s completion in 1953; perhaps what David Mogen identifies as Bradbury's inspiration for the book, Hitler's book burnings, affords little room for the comic. For whatever reasons, unlike *Chronicles*, which intersperses the solemnity of its nuclear aftermath chapters with a bit of lightness in the Walter Gripp story, Fahrenheit sustains a serious tone to the end of the book, even in its resurrectionist optimism for the future of the arts.

This optimism for the future—this notion of recivilization—is the third common element between *The Martian Chronicles* and *Fahrenheit 451* that has early cold war connections. Given such nihilistic phenomena of the cold war era as its tendencies toward censorship, its socially paranoid outlook, and its budding arms race, it may seem a strange period to give rise to any optimism. However, one of the great ironies of the period was a peripheral belief that somehow the presence of nuclear arms would, by their very capacity to bring about ultimate destruction to *all* humans, engender a very special sort of cautiousness and cooperative spirit in the world heretofore not experienced. Perhaps there was a belief that Hiroshima and Nagasaki had taught us a big enough lesson in themselves about nuclear cataclysm that we as humans would rise above our destructive tendencies and live more harmoniously. One very prominent figure who espoused this position was Dr. J. Robert Oppenheimer, the very man who headed the Los Alamos Manhattan Project. Oppenheimer would emerge as one of the most morally intriguing characters of the cold war. He was among the first in the scientific community to encourage restraint, caution, and careful deliberation in all matters regarding the pursuit of atomic energy. "There is only one future of atomic explosives that I can regard with any enthusiasm: that they should never be sued in war," he said in a 1946 address before the George Westinghouse Centennial Forum. He also refused to participate in the development of the hydrogen bomb following Los Alamos, calling such a weapon "the plague of Thebes" (Rhodes). In one of his most inspired addresses on the cooperation of art and science, Oppenheimer stated that "Both the man of science and the man of art live always at the edge of mystery, surrounded by it; both always, as the measure of their creation, have had to do with the harmonization of what is new with what is familiar, with the balance between novelty and synthesis, with the struggle to make partial order in total chaos. They can, in their work and in their lives, help themselves, help one another, and help all men."

Such a spirit of hope for renewed goodwill among men of all vocations is the optimistic vein through which society is reenvisioned following the atomic devastation of the Earth in "The Million-Year Picnic," the final chapter of *The Martian Chronicles*. Several days in the past, a rocket that had been hidden on Earth during the Great War carried William and

Alice Thomas and their children. Timothy, Michael and Robert, to Mars, presumably for a "picnic." The father admits to his inquisitive sons on this day, however, that the picnic was a front for an escape from life on Earth, where "people get lost in a mechanical wilderness" and "Wars got bigger and bigger and finally killed Earth." The father literally plans a new civilization: he blows up their rocket to avoid discovery by hostile Earthmen; he burns up all the family's printed records of their life on earth; and he now awaits, with his family, "a handful of others who'll land up in a few days. Enough to start over. Enough to turn away from all that back on Earth and strike out on a new Line." When his son Michael repeats his request to see a "Martian," the father takes his family to the canal and points to their reflections in the water. The books' last line, "The Martians started back up at them for a long, long silent time from the rippling water," is optimistic without being didactic. It suggests that this new society has in fact already begun, that it is already "marking partial order out of total chaos," as Oppenheimer suggests that cold war future needs to do. William F. Touponce believes that it is "an altogether appropriate ending" that "summarizes the experience of the reader, who has seen old illusions and values destroyed only to be replaced with new and vital ones." It also offers an image that invites the reader to extrapolate on the father's vision of "a new line" and trust the will of the colonizers for once.

Bradbury's optimism for a recivilized world is also evident in the conclusion of *Fahrenheit 451*. The seed for an optimistic ending to this dystopian work is actually planted just before the bombs strike. As Montag makes his way across the wilderness, dodging the pursuit of the mechanical hound and the helicopters, he spots the campfire of the book people. His thoughts reflect an epiphany of his transformation from a destroyer of civilization to a builder of it: "[The fire] was not burning, it was *warming*. He saw many hands held to its warmth, hands without arms, hidden in darkness. Above the hands, motionless faces that were only moved and tossed and flickered with firelight. He hadn't known fire could look this way. He had never thought in his life that it could give as well as take." This spirit of giving, of creating from the environment, is emphasized throughout the speeches given by Granger, the leader of the book preservers. In his allusion to the phoenix, which resurrects itself from the ashes of its own pyre, Granger's words reflect the new Montag, who can now see the life-sustaining properties of fire as well as its destructive powers; hopefully, Granger's words also contain hope for the American response to Hiroshima and Nagasaki: "we've got one damn thing the phoenix never had. We know the damn silly thing we just did. We know all the damn silly things we've done for a thousand years and as long as we know that and always have it around where we can see it, someday we'll stop making the goddamn funeral pyres and jumping in the middle of them." The book ends with Montag rehearsing in his mind a passage from the Book of Revelation, which he says he'll save for the reading at noon. Peter Sisario sees in this ending "a key to Bradbury's hope that the 'healing of nations' can best come about through a rebirth of man's intellect"; Sisarios's interpretation of *Fahrenheit's* ending and Oppenheimer's interpretation of mankind's necessary response to the cold war share a belief in the triumph of the benevolent side of humans.

ROBIN ANNE REID ON STYLISTIC ANALYSIS

One way of analyzing a literary work is called stylistic analysis. This sort of analysis looks closely at how a writer chooses and arranges words. A stylistic analysis can focus on the author's choice of words, grammar, or syntax (sentence structure). Usually a stylistic analysis will focus on one kind of stylistic choice (such as images) or, if on a variety of choices, on a fairly short excerpt from the work. Stylistic analysis always considers how the style contributes to the work's theme or the overall meaning.

Images are words that evoke sensory impressions: touch, taste, smell, sight, hearing. Images provide a sense of the physical reality a character experiences in a story. In realistic fiction, images are not necessarily fore-grounded, that is, given a great deal of attention. Such images often serve more as background information, meant to be taken literally for their descriptive value. But in other genres, images take on the importance they have in poetry: this is, they sometimes act as symbols, with abstract or thematic meanings as well as a literal or descriptive meaning. The term "image cluster" is used when a writer builds in a number of references to a core image.

Bradbury uses images associated with fire and burning as well as images of light and running water, throughout *Fahrenheit 451*. The novel's reliance on a specific pattern of images is discussed in detail by Donald Walt in "*Fahrenheit 451* as Symbolic Dystopia." Watt provides a careful description and analysis of how these images are associated with important characters and events throughout the novel. Images used to describe events or characters make the novel a "symbolic dystopia" for Watt, with the stylistic choices Bradbury makes resulting in a subtle and distinctive dystopian novel. Watt shows how Bradbury's use of fire imagery, with fire as both negative and positive, sets up two symbolic poles (196).

A stylistic reading can show how Bradbury brings together his three major image clusters in a short passage near the end of the novel. At this point in the story, Montag has escaped a Mechanical Hound by going into the river. Floating downstream, he is thinking about his life and the choices he has made. He previously planned to take violent action against the firemen, and has killed Captain Beatty. But after this passage, he decides not to destroy or burn anything else. Instead, he will try to preserve knowledge and life:

> He saw the moon low in the sky now. The moon there, and the light of the moon caused by what? By the sun of course. And what lights the sun? Its own fire. And the sun goes on, day after day, burning and burning. The sun and time. The sun and time and burning. Burning. The river bobbled him along gently. Burning. The sun and every clock on the earth. It all came

together and became a single thing in his mind. After a long time of floating in the river he knew why he must never burn again in his life. (140-41)

This passage has 112 words, arranged in thirteen sentences, although six of those sentences are fragments (lacking either a subject or a verb). Little action takes place: Montag is floating, passively, in the river. He sees and, by the end, he knows. The river is what moves him ("bobbled him along gently"). Since the passage lacks action verbs or, in some sentences, any verbs, the nouns attract greater attention: there are twenty-eight noun phrases, including verbs, the -ing forms of verbs, which can function as nouns or modify nouns. (There are also two verbs, "lights" and "burns" which closely parallel similar nouns.) One-quarter of the words in this passage, then, are in noun phrases.

The nouns are mostly related to Bradbury's image clusters: *sun* is used six times; *fire* and *light* are each used once. The verbal *burning* is used five times. *Moon* is used three times, and closely associated with the sun (its light comes from the sun), and *sky* is used once. *River* is used twice, and *land* and *the earth* once. The contrasting images of burning (of fires and of the sun) are brought together with the water of the river and the land. The moon, "low in the sky," is nearly touching the land, and it connects the light of the sun with the earth and water. "it all" becomes "a single thing to Montag. The other major image cluster is related to time: *time* occurs four times, *day* twice, and *clock* once. The passing of time is paralleled with the sun in two sentences: "The sun and time. The sun and time and burning."

The images in this passage have all been used before throughout the novel, to describe characters and events, and Montag's perception of them. This view of the universe, in which the opposing or destructive forces meld with the nurturing or creative forces, is a vision that results in Montag's decision to move away from destruction, even destruction for a "good cause," and toward preservation. Described in a deceptively simple style, these perceptions lead him to a new consciousness and a final decision on how he should live his life from this point on. After he leaves the river, he shortly joins the underground resistance group and commits to joining their project of memory and preservation.

SAM WELLER ON THE WRITING OF FAHRENHEIT 451

"'The Pedestrian'—even though it's not dealing with censorship—resulted in *Fahrenheit*" said Ray. "Because later, I took the pedestrian out for a walk one night again, and when he turned a corner, he bumped into this young girl named Clarisse McClellan and she took a sniff and she said, "I smell kerosene, I know who you are, and the man she bumped into said 'Who am I?' and she said, 'You're the fireman who lives up the block who burns books.'"

By 1949, the "five ladyfinger firecracker" tales were written. In 1950, Ray set out to write "the explosion." As he referred to it, that would later evolve into *Fahrenheit 451*. The earliest draft of this formative novella was titled *Long After Midnight*, and was written shortly after Ray and Maggie had moved into the Clarkson Road house. Ray had yet to transform the garage into a workable space. One afternoon, as he was roaming the UCLA library stacks, he discovered the perfect spot in which to write.

"I found the best way to inspire myself," he said, "was to go to the library in Los Angeles and rove about, pulling books from shelves, reading a line here, a paragraph there, snatching, devouring, moving on, and then suddenly writing on any handy piece of paper."

One day he heard the clatter of typewriter keys emanating from a stairwell, he went down the stairs to investigate. In the library basement he discovered a typing room with rows of desks toped with well-oiled typewriters. Each typewriter had a timer, and could be rented for a dime for each half hour. Ray had found his new office.

He went to work. In a flourish, he set out to draft the story "Long After Midnight," soon to be retitled "The Fireman." Ray made a quick outline for himself, a series of plot points he wanted to touch upon, then commenced writing madly. By the end of the first day in his new "office," he found it difficult to leave the library and ride the bus home.

In the days that followed, the writer woke at seven in the morning, took the bus to the library, and wrote until dusk. "I cannot possibly tell you what an exciting adventure it was," he recalled in the 1993 introduction to the fortieth-anniversary edition of *Fahrenheit 451*. Day after day, attacking that rentable machine, shoving dimes, pounding away like a crazed chimp, rushing upstairs to fetch more dimes, running in and out of the stacks, pulling books, scanning pages, breathing the finest pollen in the world, book dust, with which to develop literary allergies. Then racing back down blushing with love, having found some quote here, another there to shove or tuck into my burgeoning myth."

Nine days after he had started, at a total cost of $9.80 (forty-nine hours of typewriter time), Ray Bradbury had written a 25,000-word novella; it was the story of a fireman named Montag in a distant future in which firemen, instead of putting out blazes, started them. They burned books.

As with some of his other politically charged tales, such as "The Pedestrian" and "The Other Foot," many editors rejected "The Fireman." Con Congdon shopped the story to magazines such as *Harper's* and *Esquire*, but none of the major literary publications was interested. Finally, "The Fireman" was sold for three hundred dollars to Horace Gold, the editor of *Galaxy* magazine, a science fiction pulp publication, and was published in February 1951. It was the same month that Ray's third book, *The Illustrated Man*, was published. Other stories, other books, myriad film and radio projects then took hold of his attention, and Ray set "The Fireman" down for two years. He had initially hoped to include it in *The Illustrated Man* and then in *The Golden Apples of the Sun*, but decided to cut the lengthy story from both when editor Walter Bradbury though "The Fireman" unfit for both collections. *Fahrenheit 451* would have to wait two more years before it would come to life.

In 1953, in Los Angeles—and all across America, for that matter—it appeared as if economically prosperous Americans had forgotten the war years. The horrors of Nazi German had been largely brushed aside in favor of a Kodachrome culture, a new society of tract homes with white picket fences. Senator Joseph McCarthy's voice had become background noise on suburban-living-room television sets.

But not everyone was wearing red, white, and blue blinders. Despite the relative prosperity of the nation, Ray feared for the future of his two towheaded daughters. He was frightened by the new atomic world and the potential consequences of what society would do with modern technology. In addition, the "Red Scare" moved Ray to explore the alarming possibilities of a dark dystopian future.

With *The Martian Chronicles*, Ray had cleverly unified a series of his Mars-themed short stories written in the late 1940s, into a thinly veiled novel. While widely acknowledged for his mastery of the short story form, as well as for his poetic, luminous style, Ray Bradbury had yet to prove himself with a work of longer fiction. And this posed the question: Could he do it? Could Ray Bradbury's inspiration-fuelled-writing process be sustained over the course of creating a novel-length work?

"Being hit and run over by a short story is exhilarating," Ray remarked in his 1966 introduction to the book. "But how does one get hit and run over and exhilarated by such a long thing as a novel? How does one stay exhilarated day after day so the whole damn thing stays honest, so one does not begin to rationalize and spoil the process, become self-conscious and ruin the whole?"

In *The Martian Chronicles*, Ray had explored issues at that time uncommon to the science fiction genre. While the book was set fifty years in the future on the planet Mars, the stories actually confronted contemporary concerns such as racism, the anti-Communist witch hunt, environmental pollution, and nuclear war. Ray's examination of these hot-button topics would lead to the writing of *Fahrenheit 451*.

By the summer of 1952, the publishing industry was abuzz with the news about publisher Ian Ballantine and his new endeavor, Ballantine Books. Ballantine and editor Stanley

Kauffmann had left positions at Bantam Books, publisher of the paperback reprint editions of *The Martian Chronicles* and *The Illustrated Man*. Because of their affordability, the Bantam paperbacks had managed to do what had thus far eluded Doubleday's hardcover Bradbury titles—bring Ray Bradbury to a larger, mainstream audience. "Certainly the paperbacks and library-bound hardback editions became the way that the younger generation learned to love Bradbury and to see him as an American master," said Jonathan R. Eller, coauthor (with William F. Toupence) of *Ray Bradbury: The life of Fiction* a scholarly survey of Ray's publishing history.

Ray's prominence in the literary landscape was growing, and while he loved his editor, Walter Bradbury, and owed much to his creative insights, Ray was still frustrated by Doubleday's myopic vision. The publisher was insistent on marketing Ray as a science fiction writer to a science fiction audience. Ian Ballantine recognized not only the growing popularity of science fiction, but also its literary potential.

Walter Bradbury passed on "The Fireman" and agreed to allow Ray to publish it elsewhere, so long as it was not published as a novel, but within a collection of stories. Walter Bradbury did not want his prized author to write his first novel for another publisher.

In the meantime, Don Congdon spoke with Ballantine, to see if there was any interest in a new Bradbury collection. In the early 1950s, Ray Bradbury, while not yet a household name, was one of the top players in the science fiction field; he was a celebrity to fans of science fiction, horror and fantasy. *The Martian Chronicles* and *The Illustrated Man*—thanks in large part to healthy paperback sales—had sold respectably. Ray's first book of mixed fiction, *The Golden Apples of the Sun*, had received more review than all of his previous three books combined. And the reviews were largely glowing. The *New York Times* stated, "He writes in a style that seems to have been nourished on poets and fabulists of the Irish Literary Renaissance. And he is wonderfully adept at getting to the heart of the story, without talking all day long about it and around it."

In Bradbury, publisher Ian Ballantine recognized the potential for much more. Ballantine wanted Ray Bradbury to write a book for his company—a company that would break new ground in publishing by offering, simultaneously, both paperback and hardcover books. After discussions, in late 1952, Ray signed with Ballantine to write a collection that would include the novella "The Fireman," to be written with an additional 25,000 words. All parties involved agreed that the story could be elaborated on. The advance for this new book was five thousand dollars. Though his stature as an American writer had grown dramatically, Ray was still financially strapped, and the advance from Ballantine was welcome.

By now, the two Bradbury girls, Susan and Ramona, were aged three and two, respectively. Full of toddler energy, they liked to romp about the three-bedroom home on Clarkson Road and play in the backyard, where there was a man-made pond. The girls especially adored watching the tadpoles in the pond, and inside the garage, which Ray had finally converted into an office, Ray tried to work as the girls called to him from outside the window. The girls threw pebbles at the garage window and their father giggled as he typed. A playful man, easily distracted and ever the child at heart, Ray could hardly ignore the pleas of his kids, so he almost always gave in and ran outside to ply. But he had a book to write and he needed a real office. However, with a meager annual income and monthly mortgage payments, the Bradburys could ill afford it. In addition, they had bought a dishwasher and a dining room set on installment. When Ray Bradbury opened the first dishwasher bill and saw the amount going to interest, he was alarmed and swore to finish the payments quickly. So he again returned to UCLA this time to finish his book for Ballantine.

Another round of days and dimes ensued. Ray Bradbury joined the typists in the typewriter rental room to add 25,00 new words to "The Fireman." In revising his novella, he knew he had to consult his original story, "The Fireman," but at the same time he didn't want to over intellectualize his approach to writing; it ran counter to his usual style.

"I feared for refiring the book and rebaking the characters," noted Ray. "I am a passionate, not intellectual writer, which means my characters must plunge ahead of me to live the story. If my intellect caught up with them too swiftly, the whole adventure might mire down in self doubt and endless mind play."

Despite these concerns, Ray Bradbury was determined to turn "The Fireman" into a short novel. However, the story would be just a center piece, surrounded by other stories, to adhere to his agreement with Doubleday.

As he wrote the book, he determined not to consult the original story. "I just let the characters talk to me," he said, remembering his first hours writing *Fahrenheit 451* and invoking the age-old writer's cliché. "I didn't write *Fahrenheit 451*, it wrote me." The plot line was still the same, the characters still in place. Fireman Montag; his pill-popping wife Mildred; Clarisse McClellan who told Montag about the power of the books that he burned each night. There were some minor changes. Fire Chief Leahy became Fire Chief Beatty, certain scenes were tossed out, others were fleshed out, the language waxed more poetic, and the story expanded as Ray wrote. Additionally, he hyped up the fire and sun symbolism. Once again, in just nine days, he finished, this time producing his first draft of the book.

RAY BRADBURY ON EARLY INFLUENCES

"Of what is past, or passing, or to come."

That says it all.

The last line of William Butler Yeats's hypnotic poem "Sailing to Byzantium."

It describes the entire history of mankind on Earth.

It tells the whole history of science fiction in a few incredible words.

For history and science fiction are inseparable.

Poppycock?

No, humanity's truth.

For all that human beings have ever thought about is the future.

Hiding in caves, discovering fire, building cities—all of these were science-fictional endeavors. We can see the depiction of possible futures scrawled on cave walls in southern France where the first science-fiction tales illustrated how to find, kill, and eat the wild beasts.

The problems that faced primitive man had to be solved. They dreamed answers to dire questions; that is the essence of the fiction that becomes science. Once a vivid dream was realized in their heads, they were able to act on it. So the creatures of old time planned for tomorrow and tomorrow and tomorrow. What is true of them certainly is true of us. We wonder about tomorrow morning, tomorrow evening, and the day after that so as to plan our schools, marriages, and careers. Everything that we do has to be imagined first.

In the castle walls at Pierrefond are embedded cannonballs that signified the destruction of walled cities forever. The land barons who inhabited them had dreamed walls to a certain height and a certain thickness. Their fictional dreams had reared the castles, and now the invention of gunpowder and the cannon was a fiction made real that brought the castles down, to change history.

When Cortes invaded Mexico, for every one of his conquistadors who died, one hundred of Montezuma's men were destroyed because of a dream of destruction, a fictional concept that made a reality of the guns the Spaniards carried.

In the further fictions that became dreams in American history, the invention of the repeating rifle and the Gatling gun did away with the Indian tribes as we moved across the country.

All, all of it fictions that became sciences and technology. I must have realized this at a very young age when I skimmed through the pages of *Science and Invention*, which was starting to make great leaps into future space. Covers of the old science-fiction magazines were filled with incredible cities that towered skyward.

I looked around at my small town, Waukegan, Illinois, and found something horribly missing.

I began to imagine those impossible cities and draw them in place.

Two amazing things happened in my ninth and tenth years: *Buck Rogers in the 25th Century* appeared in American newspapers in October 1929, the start of the Great Depression. That one strip's concussion shook me into a new life.

In that strip I saw Buck Rogers stagger from a cave, where he had slept for five hundred years in suspended animation to see Wilma Deering flash through the sky, firing a rocket pistol. Looking up, Buck Rogers found himself in a new age.

That one comic strip transported me into the future. I began to collect Buck Rogers adventures and never returned from that long journey into tomorrow.

The second collision occurred when I discovered Edgar Rice Burrough's *John Carter, Warlord of Mars.* His Mars was a fantastic creation totally impossible but totally acceptable to a lunatic ten-year-old.

John Carter instructed me to stand on my summer-night lawn and look up a the sky, lift my arms out toward the red planet and cry, Mars, take me home! Instantly, as with John Carter, my soul slid from my body, rushed across space, landed on Mars, and I never came back.

From that future, age twelve, I began to write about further futures, because I found the world around me terribly Baptist plain.

Then the Chicago World's Fair, 1933, exploded. I walked, stunned, through that world of fantastic colors and shapes, where the city of the future was actually built. Entranced by the encounter, I refused to go home at night. My parents had to drag me onto the train to ship me north to Waukegan.

Then I discovered the most incredible truth: The people who had built the fair were going to tear it down two years later.

Idiots! I though. How stupid that you could build a future and then, mindlessly, destroy all those beauties.

I raced to my nickel tablet and began to draw architectural blueprints of possible cities and outrageous buildings in some reborn time.

Simultaneously I wrote sequels to the novels of Edgar Rice Burroughs and soon learned the truth of what Admiral Byrd had said when leaving for the North Pole:

"Jules Verne leads me."

So Jules Verne, with Edgar Rice Burroughs and Buck Rogers, led me on my incredible trip into myself.

This conglomeration was fused when I encountered Mr. Electrico.

Mr. Electrico was a carnival magician who performed on one Labor Day weekend. In his electric chair, he was electrocuted each night and reached with his sword of blue fire to tap kids in the front row. He pressed his sword to my brow, filled me with electric juice, and cried, "Live forever!"

I thought, Boy, that's great! How do you *do* that?

I went to see him the next day to find out how to live forever.

We sat on the beach and talked and suddenly he said that he had met me a long time ago, that I had lived before. He said that I was his best friend in the First World War and had been wounded and died in his arms in Ardennes Forest outside Paris in October 1918. And here I was, back in the world, with a new face, a new name, but the soul shining out of my eyes was the soul of his dead friend.

"Welcome back to the world!" Mr. Electrico said.

Why he said this to me, I do not know.

Perhaps he saw something of the strange future in my face. Something I could not see myself.

On the way home from the carnival grounds, I stood by the carousel to watch the horses whirl, and hear "Beautiful Ohio" played on the calliope while tears rained down my face.

I knew that something important had happened that day.

Within weeks I began to write short stories combining Burroughs, Verne, and L. Frank Baum and his wonderful Oz.

I have written every day for the rest of my life after that last day with Mr. Electrico.

Works by Ray Bradbury

Dark Carnival, 1947.

The Martian Chronicles, 1950 .

The Illustrated Man, 1951.

Fahrenheit 451, 1953.

The Golden Apples of the Sun, 1953.

Switch on the Night, 1955.

The October Country, 1955.

Dandelion Wine, 1957.

A Medicine for Melancholy, 1959.

R Is for Rocket, 1962.

Something Wicked This Way Comes, 1962.

The Machineries of Joy, 1964.

The Autumn People, 1965.

The Vintage Bradbury, 1965.

S Is for Space, 1966.

Tomorrow Midnight, 1966.

Twice Twenty-Two, 1966.

Any Friend of Nicholas Nickleby's Is a Friend of Mine, 1968.

The Halloween Tree, 1968.

I Sing the Body Electric!, 1969.

When Elephants Last in the Dooryard Bloomed, 1973.

Long After Midnight, 1976.

Where Robot Mice and Robot Men Run Round in Robot Towns, 1977.

The Stories of Ray Bradbury, 1980.

The Haunted Computer and the Android Pope, 1981.

Complete Poems, 1982.

A Memory of Murder, 1984.

Death Is a Lonely Business, 1985.

Bradbury on Stage: A Chrestomathy of His Plays, 1988.

The Toynbee Convector, 1988.

A Graveyard for Lunatics, 1990.

Zen in the Art of Writing, 1990.

Yestermorrow: Obvious Answers to Impossible Futures, 1991.

Green Shadow, White Whale, 1992.

Quicker Than the Eye, 1996.

Dogs Think That Every Day Is Christmas, 1997.

With Cat for Comforter, 1997.

Ahmed and the Oblivion Machines, 1998.

Driving Blind, 1998.

From the Dust Returned, 2001.

One More for the Road, 2002.

They Have Not Seen The Stars: The Collected Poetry of Ray Bradbury, 2002.

Bradbury Stories: 100 of His Most Celebrated Tales, 2003.

It Came from Outer Space, 2003.

Let's All Kill Constance, 2003.

The Cat's Pajamas, 2004.

Conversations with Ray Bradbury, 2004.

Bradbury Speaks: Too Soon from the Cave, Too Far from the Stars, 2005.

A Sound of Thunder and Other Stories, 2005.

Annotated Bibliography

Bradbury, Ray, "Ray Bradbury: Poet of Fantastic Fiction" with Jeffrey M. Elliot in *Science Fiction Voices*, number 2, Borgo Press (1979) pages 20–29.

This interview with Bradbury interview focuses on the particular characteristics of Bradbury's distinctive style.

Guffey, George R., "*Fahrenheit 451* and the 'Cubby-Hole Editors' of Ballantine Books" in *Coordinates: Placing Science Fiction and Fantasy*, edited by George E. Slusser, Eric S. Rabkin, and Robert Scholes, Southern Illinois University Press (1983) pages 99–106.

Guffey's piece examines Bradbury's own brushes with censorship, and the earlier development of the theme of free expression in his earlier stories.

Huntington, John, "Utopian and Anti-Utopian Logic: H.G. Wells and His Successors" in *Science Fiction Studies* 9, no. 2 (July 1982) pages 122–146.

Huntington contextualizes the novel in a broader scheme of dystopian literature. Particular emphasis and scrutiny are placed on Bradbury's use of contradiction in the novel.

Hugh-Jones, Stephen, "Bradburies" in *New Statesman* LXVIII, no. 1749 (September 18, 1964) page 406.

This brief but enlightening review details the versatility with which Bradbury moves between genres.

McLaughlin, John J., "Science Fiction Theatre" in *The Nation* 200, no. 4 (January 25, 1965) pages 92–94.

McLaughlin's review favorable examines the importance of the novel's political content.

Moore, Everett T., "A Rationale for Bookburners: A Further Word from Ray Bradbury" in *ALA Bulletin*, vol 55, number 5 (May 1961) pages: 403-4.

This early review, has a more topical analysis of the relevance of Bradbury's theme of censorship.

Sisario, Peter, "A Study of the Allusions in Bradbury's *Fahrenheit 451*" in *English Journal* 59, no. 2 (February 1970) pages: 201–205, 212.

Here Sisario traces the many different citations in the novel back to their sources with emphasis on Bradbury's use of intertextuality.

Slusser, George Edgar, "*Fahrenheit 451*" in *The Bradbury Chronicles*, Borgo Press (1977) pages 52-54.

Slusser compares the novel to the story, "The Fireman," on which it was based, noting in particular Bradbury's changes.

Spencer, Susan, "The Post-Apocalyptic Library: Oral and Literate Culture in *Fahrenheit 451* and *A Canticle for Leibowitz*" in *Extrapolation* 32, no. 4, (Winter 1991) pages 331–342.

Spencer's piece is a useful examination of the thematic resemblances between two science fiction novels, both marked by their tendency to criticize oral culture as being antagonistic to textual culture.

Touponce, William F., "Some Aspects of Surrealism in the Work of Ray Bradbury" in *Extrapolation* 25, no. 3 (Fall 1984) pages 228–238.

Touponce, a respected science fiction scholar, writes of the similarities and possible influences linking Bradbury's style in general to the artistic innovations of the French Surrealists and their American successors.

Watt, Donald, "Burning Bright: *Fahrenheit 451* as Symbolic Dystopia" in *Ray Bradbury*, edited by Martin H. Greenberg and Joseph D. Olander, Taplinger Publishing Company (1980) pages 195–213.

Watt's piece is a useful study of Bradbury's use of figures and poetic rhetoric in the development of his setting, in time and place.

Wood, Diane S., "Bradbury and Atwood: Exile as Rational Decision" in *The Literature of Emigration and Exile*, edited by James Whitlark and Wendell Aycock, Texas Tech University Press (1992) pages 131–142.

As indicated by the title of her essay, Wood elucidates the novel in light of a reading of *The Handmaid's Tale*, by Margaret Atwood.

Contributors

Harold Bloom is Sterling Professor of the Humanities at Yale University. He is the author of 30 books, including *Shelley's Mythmaking* (1959), *The Visionary Company* (1961), *Blake's Apocalypse* (1963), *Yeats* (1970), *A Map of Misreading* (1975), *Kabbalah and Criticism* (1975), *Agon: Toward a Theory of Revisionism* (1982), *The American Religion* (1992), *The Western Canon* (1994), and *Omens of Millennium: The Gnosis of Angels, Dreams, and Resurrection* (1996). *The Anxiety of Influence* (1973) sets forth Professor Bloom's provocative theory of the literary relationships between the great writers and their predecessors. His most recent books include *Shakespeare: The Invention of the Human* (1998), a 1998 National Book Award finalist, *How to Read and Why* (2000), *Genius: A Mosaic of One Hundred Exemplary Creative Minds* (2002), *Hamlet: Poem Unlimited* (2003), *Where Shall Wisdom Be Found?* (2004), and *Jesus and Yahweh: The Names Divine* (2005). In 1999, Professor Bloom received the prestigious American Academy of Arts and Letters Gold Medal for Criticism. He has also received the International Prize of Catalonia, the Alfonso Reyes Prize of Mexico, and the Hans Christian Andersen Bicentennial Prize of Denmark.

Michael Cisco holds a PhD. in English literature from New York University and specializes in the study of ante-bellum American literature and philosophy. He is author of *Supernatural Embarrassment: Five Landings in American Literature*, and the novels *The Divinity Student* and *The Tyrant*.

Peter Sisario has written reviews in *English Journal*

Wayne L. Johnson is the author of *Ray Bradbury*. He has contributed articles and essays to numerous journals, and has contributed to the collection *Critical Encounters: Writers and Themes in Science Fiction*.

William F. Touponce is professor of English, adjunct professor of American Studies, and a member of the Institute for American Thought at Indiana University. He has also written on Frank Herbert and Isaac Asimov.

David Mogen holds a PhD. in English Literature from the University of Colorado at Boulder, and has taught at Colorado State University. He is the author of *Wilderness Visions*, a study of the frontier as a concept in American science fiction.

Kevin Hoskinson has taught at Lorain County Community College where he is a part of programs for student success. His teaching and scholarly research focuses upon 20th century American literature as well as Irish drama.

Robin Anne Reid has written on Arthur C. Clarke. She is Assistant Professor of Literature and Languages at Texas A&M University-Commerce, Texas.

Sam Weller has written for *Publishers Weekly* and the *Chicago Tribune Magazine*. He teaches at Columbia College in Chicago, including a course dedicated exclusively to Bradbury currently available.

Ray Bradbury is the acclaimed author of *Fahrenheit 451*, *The Martian Chronicles*, and numerous other works. Among his many awards are the Jules Verne Award and the Valentine Davies Award. Many of his short stories have been selected to the *Best American Short Story* collections.

Acknowledgments

Peter Sisaro, "A Study of the Allusions in Bradbury's Fahrenheit 451," in *English Journal*, Vol. 59, No. 2, February 1970. Copyright © 1970 by the National Council of Teachers of English. Reprinted by permission.

Wayne L. Johnson "Machineries of Joy and Sorrow," in *Ray Bradbury*, pp. 85–88. © 1980 by Frederick Ungar Publishing Co. Reprinted by permission

William Touponce, *Ray Bradbury and the Poetics of Reverie, Fantasy, Science Fiction, and the Reader*, UMI Research Press, © 1984. Reprinted by permission of William F. Touponce.

"*Fahrenheit 451*" by David Mogen. From *Ray Bradbury*, pp. 105–108. © 1986 by Twayne Publishers. Reprinted by permission of the Gale Group.

Kevin Hoskinson, From *Extrapolation* 36, no. 4. © 1995 by Kent State University Press. (Originally published as "The Martian Chronicles and *Fahrenheit 451*: Ray Bradbury's Cold War Novels".) Reprinted with permission of the Kent State University Press.

"*Fahreneit 451*" by Robin Anne Reid. From *Ray Bradbury: A Critical Companion*, pp. 60–62. © 2000 by Greenwood Press. Reproduced with permission of Greenwood Publishing Group, Inc., Westport, CT.

"*Fahreneit 451*" by Sam Well. From *The Bradbury Chronicles: The Life of Ray Bradbury*, pp. 200–205. © 2005 by Sam Weller. Reprinted by permission of HarperCollins Publishers.

Every effort has been made to contact the owners of copyrighted material and secure copyright permission. Articles appearing in this volume generally appear much as they did in their original publication with few or no editorial changes. In some cases foreign language text has been removed from the original essay. Those interested in locating the original source will find bibliographic information in the bibliography and acknowledgments sections of this volume.

Index

honesty, relationship with Clarisse and, 49
Hope. *See* Optimism
horror, mixing of nature and technology as, 56–57
hound. *See* Mechanical Hound
humanity, 17, 25–26, 36–37
Huntington, John, 56–58
Huxley, Aldous, 13, 65

I

idealism, tyranny and, 65
ideas, printed matter as, 33
Illustrated Man, 10, 11, 75
imagery, stylistic analysis of, 71–74
indifference of Guy toward Mildred, 19
individualism, 22–23, 28. *See also* conformism
influences on Ray Bradbury, 79–82
intellectualism, criticism of, 63
intellectuals, limitations of, 33
irony
   of Captain Beatty's speeches, 24–30, 63
   false enlightenment and, 59–60
   use of books as, 48–49
"It Came From Outer Space," 10

J

Job, Book of, 52
John Carter, Warlord of Mars, influence of, 81, 82
Johnson, Samuel, 31

L

Language
   manipulation and, 16, 58–59
   stylistic analysis of, 71–74
Latimer, Hugh, 51
lies, happiness as, 21–22, 50–51
Life of Johnson, 31, 49
Lilies of the Field, 52
Lilliputians, 30, 48–49
literature, 43–46, 47–51

Long After Midnight, 74
love, 19, 21
Lovecraft, H.P., 10

M

machines. *See* technology
Manhattan Project, 67, 69
manipulation, language and, 16, 58–59
marriage, as sham, 19
Martian Chronicles
   Arizona landscape and, 9
   description of, 53, 62
   issues in, 76–77
   optimism and, 69–70
   writing of, 10, 11
McCarthyism, 12, 63, 65, 76
McClellan, Clarisse
   character overview of, 14, 20
   Guy's feelings for, 34–35
   liquidation of, 24
   reverie and, 61
Mechanical Hound, 29, 42–43, 55
media, government and, 16
memorization of literature, 43–46
memory
   books and, 39
   entrapment in, 62
   living libraries and, 43–46
mental illness, criticism of state and, 40–41
metamorphosis as theme, 54–55
metaphors, firemen as, 63
"Meteor", 10
Miller, Arthur, 12
"Million-Year Picnic", 69–70
Mogen, David, 68
Montag, Guy
   character overview of, 14
   consciousness raising of, 54–55
   introduction to, 18
   reading to Mildred and, 31
   thoughtfulness and, 34–35
Montag, Mildred
   character overview of, 14

94